BY THE SAME AUTHOR

SWEDEN: THE MIDDLE WAY

THIS IS DEMOCRACY

COLLECTIVE BARGAINING

IN SCANDINAVIA

BY MARQUIS W. CHILDS

NEW HAVEN · YALE UNIVERSITY PRESS · 1938

38·27852

FOR

O. K. BOVARD

WHOSE COURAGE AND INSIGHT HAVE INSPIRED
A GENERATION OF REPORTERS

ACKNOWLEDGMENTS

I have written this book primarily from firsthand interviews and observations, as a reporter, and I am therefore indebted to an overwhelming number of persons who were kind enough to give me their time. Since it would be impossible to express individual thanks to all of these I must content myself with acknowledging the special patience and kindness of a few. Two distinguished economists, Professor Bertil Ohlin and Professor Gunnar Myrdal, sought to save me from the grosser errors of interpretation. Mr. Torsten Gårdlund, a young economist in the university of Stockholm and already active in trade-union councils, has been kind enough to read the manuscript and I am deeply indebted to him for his criticism and suggestions. For their consideration and courtesy I wish to thank Dr. Sigfrid Hansson of the Social Board in the Swedish Ministry of Social Affairs; Mr. Oscar Falkman of the Boliden Corporation; Mr. Finn Moe of Arbeiderbladet *in Oslo; Mr. Marcus Wallenberg of Stockholms Enskilda Banken; and Captain Lindman and Miss Jungbeck of the Swedish Traffic Association. I am particularly indebted to Miss Elsa Britta Hansson for her kindness in putting me in touch with firsthand sources of information. Once again I am indebted to the American-Swedish News Exchange and its officers, Mr. Nils Horney in Stockholm and Mr. Naboth Hedin in New York, with special thanks to Mrs. Horney for the courtesy and kindness she showed the American invaders. I am in the debt of all our diplomatic officers in Scandinavia for their unfailing consideration and interest and particularly to Mrs. J. Borden Harriman, the Minister to Norway. In America Professor E. Wight Bakke, through his critical reading of the manuscript, and Mr. Eugene Davidson, through his patience and tact as editor, have given invaluable assistance. My thanks are due to Miss Eleanor*

Powell for assistance in preparing the manuscript. Without the aid of my wife, who has been in many respects a collaborator, giving unsparingly of her time and energy, and contributing a keen critical perspective as well as infinite patience in the details of research and translation, I could not have completed the book.

I must add the formal postscript that I alone am responsible for errors of fact and interpretation which may occur despite the advice and assistance so generously accorded me.

CONTENTS

ILLUSTRATIONS

INTRODUCTION

IN this book I have tried to give an idea of what labor has achieved through the process of collective bargaining in the northern democracies—Sweden, Norway, and Denmark. While it is in no sense a history, some background is essential to an understanding of how organized workers have gained their present position of power in Scandinavia. It is a quick view, a surface view, but one which I hope will be clear in all its implications to those Americans who are just now concerned over the status of labor and the problem of trade-union organization.

In two ways labor has bargained. First, there has been a never-ceasing effort for fifty years or more to raise the level of real wages, and there is evidence, statistical and tangible, to show a considerable measure of success. Judged by indexes of food consumption, health, age of dwellings, use of leisure time, real wages, the living standard is high, certainly in comparison with other European countries. But comparison of national living standards is at best impressionistic and not infrequently such comparisons are prejudiced by a childish chauvinism. Judged by their own past, Scandinavian workers have made substantial gains.

Second, labor has bargained at the polls for political power, and so successfully that labor majorities govern the three countries. By patient, painstaking steps the workers have created their own political organization, Socialist in character, and through this means they have come into control, nominal control at least, of the state. Independent of the older political parties, the Laborites in Scandinavia have nevertheless frequently coöperated with Liberals and Farmers in the course of their evolutionary rise. They have obtained through their organized political power a wide range of social services and benefits, and in this way they have also improved their status. Some economists believe that labor has gained more by this method than by wage bargaining.

Americans disturbed by the seemingly inevitable conflicts

growing out of the rise of a mass labor movement have cherished the illusion that beyond the seas, in Great Britain and Scandinavia, the very fact of collective bargaining and an established body of labor law is somehow an insurance against strikes. Quite the opposite is true as is shown by a comparative study covering a period of ten years just published by the International Labor Office at Geneva.

For the decade from 1927 through 1936 the country with the most man-days lost per thousand workers in industry as a result of wage disputes, this study shows, was Norway where the average was 3,176. Next came Sweden with 1,818 days and Denmark was third with an average of 935. This is evidence indeed of the right to carry a wage dispute to the ultimate length of a strike or a lockout. (These figures include stoppages initiated by employers as well as by employees.) Labor Party leaders in power in the Scandinavian countries are concerned over the frequency of strikes and lockouts, since such dislocations threaten the plans of governments trying to achieve a more stable economy. But no responsible politician of any major party would be likely to suggest any drastic curb on the right to strike.

Labor in Scandinavia, as these same figures indicate, is far too militant for any such move to succeed. How nearly the Labor Office statistics are a measure of the militancy of Scandinavian trade unions it is difficult to say. Certainly they show that wage scales have not been arrived at without a struggle.

The present view, on the surface at least, is a hopeful one. But when one takes a longer look, the possibility suggests itself that these labor governments may be only a transitory manifestation of the particular phase of industrial development that these countries have now reached; the result of singularly fortunate circumstances. With new technological development, industrialization of those countries that are still "backward," sharper competition in the world market, this orderly structure may give way; and labor, having held power over the political but not the major economic forces of the state, may be swept aside.

There is the example of Great Britain where in at least one or two fields high wage standards based upon voluntary agreements renewed through many decades have now given way to state regulation intended to save at least a minimum scale. And in Great Britain labor's political organization has fallen to a state so low that even the most optimistic leaders cannot foresee a time when they will be returned to power.

For many decades a system emphasizing voluntary wage negotiations and wage contracts, between trade union and employer representatives, functioned with comparatively few interruptions in Great Britain. Systematic and orderly collective bargaining was a part of the industrial process. But after 1918 the so-called backward nations, in Central Europe and Asia, began to develop their own textile mills, buying machines from Great Britain and the United States. The British no longer held unrivaled dominance over the markets of India, China, and South America.

Labor costs in Japanese textile mills were much lower than in the Manchester area. British mills began to shut down. Mill owners were in despair. Here and there, particularly in towns where there was only one industry, they called their workers together and showed them the books. The choice was to close down or pay wages lower than the union scale. The men agreed to take a cut. This began to happen more and more frequently until demoralization threatened the entire industry.

It was at this point that spokesmen for both unions and employers approached the government. They asked for a law that would save in part, at least, standards painstakingly built up through the years. As a result the Cotton Manufacturing Industry Act was passed in 1934 providing for compulsory minimum wage scales to be fixed by joint application to the Ministry of Labor of organizations representing both parties. Under the law a board is then appointed to fix the scale. Penalties are provided for failure to pay the minimum. While the textile industry is an extreme example, the same forces of world competition have had a marked effect in other fields.

A significant question arises when one contemplates the tactics of Scandinavian trade unions in the light of English events. The question that comes to mind is whether or not the reformist trade-union movement is merely one phenomenon in a phase of the cycle of industrialization. It comes into being on the upward swing, with the increase in wealth that comes out of industrialization; in this phase of expansion the trade unions force a marked rise in real wages; through political pressure they achieve distinct social benefits.

But can this structure be sustained in a declining phase? It may be said that these questions are pertinent only to Great Britain, dependent upon a world export trade and the existence of a vast colonial empire. Yet in Sweden there are certain parallels. The rise of the trade unions and the growth of social services have come with the rapid increase in wealth that industrialization has brought about in the past fifty years. Before that time Sweden was a poor country with a low standard of living. And as in Britain, Swedish industry is in no small degree dependent upon the export market. At the present moment Soviet Russia is completing new steel plants capable of producing a high-grade tool steel such as in the past has been obtained from Germany, Sweden, and the United States. However small this may have been, here is a market that is gone. And there is no assurance that other industrially backward countries will not sooner or later push this same process of industrialization.

In Sweden there is increasing concentration on the home market with an effort to build up farm purchasing power. It may be possible to avoid the worst effects of world competition in highly industrialized fields. Only with time will it be possible to give any final answers. Nevertheless it is important to realize how dependent the whole structure of trade unionism is upon the fluctuating currents of world trade.

Labor leaders in Scandinavia are well aware of the British example. They realize that it is necessary to broaden the base of the political movement that labor has created and to consider the national economy, both for immediate objectives and in the long view, from a far more generous perspective than they have held in the past. European events of the past five years have been deeply disturbing: above all what happened in Germany in 1933 and in Austria in 1934, the annihilation of labor in two Western nations where once it was strongly and coherently organized.

Labor leaders in Scandinavia, as all over the world, have been profoundly troubled by these events. They have seemed to raise a fundamental question: Is there a choice for labor in the world today between revolution and reform? In Sweden and Denmark the labor movement has been almost from the beginning reformist, parliamentary, gradualist. But in Norway a revolutionary impulse was for many years dominant and it is therefore very significant that the Social-Democratic party has recently adopted a reformist program which includes aid to private industry, subsidies to farmers, an appeal to the middle class.

The more radical Laborites in Scandinavia, and particularly in Norway, revert again and again to the disaster that occurred in Vienna in February, 1934. The Austrian proletariat, it is generally agreed, was the most thoroughly disciplined and the best armed in the world. Yet in a conflict they were helpless before the artillery, tanks, and machine guns of the ruling class. After all it is impossible to keep a tank in one's basement or an airplane in the kitchen. Is it not obvious that the ruling class will always manage to maintain control over these superior armaments, if necessary by subsidizing an élite of the soldiery, a praetorian guard? These are the thoughts that trouble Norwegian labor leaders as they seek to shape a reformist policy, realizing that within the rank and file there is still a revolutionary impulse, intolerant of gradualism and parliamentary tactics.

In Sweden and Denmark the problem of the leaders is quite another one. Far more conservative by background and experience, they have come into office in an interval of prosperity. The tendency is to let well enough alone. And yet many leaders both within and without the government are aware that if major reforms are not undertaken, a new crisis may find the Socialists helpless. In that event a reaction would almost certainly occur and it would be years before the party could overcome the resulting disillusion and distrust. Leaders who have grown up in the tradition of bargaining for small gains find it difficult to take a longer view; the small necessities of the present obscure the future.

It is clearly a harsh dilemma. Advance, progress, is essential. But the question is how far can this advance go. At what point will middle-class and farm support be withdrawn? And at what point will the government meet the serious challenge of that owning minority most likely to be affected by reform? Sharpening this dilemma is a new factor: the shadow over the Scandinavian peninsula of Nazi Germany. Every error, every weakness, every hesitation and show of doubt, is scored off against democracy and Social-Democratic policy, while behind a censorship ruthlessly enforced, Germany presents to her neighbors a façade of national unity and achievement that is impressive no matter what the degree of its falsity.

There is everywhere the sense that this is a changed world, one that bears but slight relation to 1927 and scarcely any at all to 1917. The effort of labor politicians to adjust to the threat of world Fascism is extremely interesting, and especially so in Sweden. If I have devoted what may seem to be a disproportionate part of this book to that country, it is not alone because it contains what is, relative to population, the strongest trade-union movement in the world; in many respects the Swedish labor movement is also the soundest and most intelligent manifestation of the capacity of organized workers to govern a modern state.

How much significance the experience of these small countries with their homogeneous populations has for America, it is difficult to say. There are many who would dismiss them as examples so special as to be meaningless; irrelevant to the problems of larger nations. Certainly they will not serve as a model for a country of continental size with a highly diverse people. No one would be so naïve as to suggest that their laws, their customs, could be taken over bodily in America.

But neither do I think that their experience can be dismissed as without meaning. They are democracies with all the virtues and all the faults inherent in the democratic form. The fate of the world will not turn on the destiny of these northern democracies. But nevertheless, the success or failure of the experiment that is going forward in the Scandinavian peninsula—and all forms of human society are in the last analysis experimental—will have no little bearing on the future of the Western world.

There are those, of course, who speak with a kind of pitying scorn of a "middle way." (In an earlier work on these same northern democracies the "middle way" was defined as a "course between the absolute socialization of Russia and the end development of capitalism in America." "In Russia before the modifications introduced by Josef Stalin . . . the rulers of the state tried to make all of life conform to an idea, an ideal. In the United States the profit motive was put above every other consideration and it worked to the end of blind self-destruction.") They would apparently accept nothing less than the apocalyptic overturn of the whole order of society. At the opposite extreme of the political spectrum are those who set themselves against any change whatsoever; living in a confused dream of a past that never was, they are as far removed from reality as those wishful thinkers who project themselves into an impossible utopia.

In both of these attitudes, it seems to me, there is no little evidence of psycho-pathology. It may represent a perversion of the religious impulse; a determination to achieve here and now, day after tomorrow, that impossible perfection which in so many religions, particularly among primitive peoples, is the focus of distant and unearthly hope. Human values painfully built up through the centuries count for nothing with these apocalypsts who stop at no sacrifice to achieve their impossible heaven on earth. In its cruder manifestations, as in Germany, the reversion to a dark and bloody primitivism, a mythical past created by propaganda on a mass production basis, is terrifyingly swift. In an age in which such a reversion is possible the sanity of a people who recognize the limitations as well as the potentialities of human society is welcome indeed.

M. W. C.

THIS IS DEMOCRACY

CHAPTER I

HOW LABOR HAS ORGANIZED

THE trade unions in the three Scandinavian countries owe their present power to many years of patient, painstaking effort; education, propaganda, and, most important of all, an unceasing campaign for new members, a campaign in which not infrequently harsh measures have been employed. This is the contemporary phase, this gradual growth to a point of impressive numerical strength. It did not come until after earlier attempts to take the citadel of industry by storm had ended in failure and disillusion, what seemed at the time to be disaster.

Broadly speaking there have been three stages in this development. In the first phase skilled workers sought by organization to build some defense against the devastating effects of the machine and the horrors of the industrial revolution. If nothing more, the instinct of self-preservation would have led men into these early organizations that were often of necessity secret, always naïve, and rarely of any avail against the evils of the time. The leaders of those primitive organizations in the 'seventies and 'eighties were regarded by society in general as criminals and for their passionate devotion to "the cause" they not infrequently suffered a painful and prolonged martyrdom.

As one traces the course of the industrial revolution in first one part of the world and then another, it appears to have struck almost like a plague, bringing with it the most fearful hardship and suffering. England is, of course, the classic example. There in the first "workshop of the world," a whole new class of the dispossessed endured appalling degradation and all according to the rules of the classical economists. What seems extraordinary is that the onset of this disease was accepted with complacence, its most dreadful symptoms taken as evidence of progress and growth. While it struck late in Scandinavia and with somewhat less virulence than in Great Britain, it nevertheless made itself felt with a sharp and unrelenting cruelty. Workers were driven into organizations that were scarcely more than a desperate defensive alliance.

In 1872 the bricklayers of Copenhagen went out on strike. They wanted to hold a meeting on the Common for the peaceful purpose of raising money in support of their strike and to demand the appointment of a Minister of Labor and other reforms. But the meeting was banned and three leaders, Pio, Brix, and Geleff, were sentenced to long prison terms. In Sweden in the 'seventies and 'eighties there were a number of bitter strikes by workers more or less unorganized, whose wretched lot drove them to this drastic form of protest. A young doctor, Anton Nyström, who had taken an interest in the early workers' organizations and had tried, unsuccessfully, to mediate a strike, was denounced and ostracized by his class. It was contrary to nature that workers should band together, contrary to the natural laws of the classical economists who held that the "labor market" should be free in order that the price of "hands" might find its "natural" level.

The first trade unions derived in part from the desire of craftsmen, highly-skilled workers, to protect their trade from the destructive impact of the machine. It was in part a carry-over from the guilds which before the industrial revolution had enforced an iron-clad labor monopoly, regulating the admittance of apprentices and virtually all other factors in connection with the conduct of the crafts.

The *gesällskap,* organizations of journeymen within the craft guilds, persisted in a few instances as benevolent societies, providing illness and death benefits. It was in 1846 that the guilds were dissolved by the free trade law of that year. Outstanding benevolent societies that survived the transition period were those made up of compositors and bookbinders.

After 1846 the social isolation of the craftsmen called forth educational associations that grew partly out of the interest of liberal philanthropists. Craftsmen, factory workers, and upperclass intellectuals all participated in these curious societies. In the 'sixties they debated reform projects of various kinds. A good example of this transition form was the Stockholm Machine

Workers' Association of 1875, dominated by liberal employers and united by ceremonial and ritualistic ties. Strindberg in his great novel, *Röda Rummet,* published in 1879, gives a vivid and somewhat humorous picture of such a workers' association, one in which upper-class intellectuals did all the talking.

All this belongs to the beginning phase of Swedish trade unionism. During the early 'eighties, with the arrival of such leaders as August Palm and socialism, these liberal associations either became class-conscious trade unions or they disappeared. It remains true nevertheless that the desire to safeguard a craft monopoly is a factor in the trade-union movement of today, one of the problems, as will be seen, that troubles present-day labor leaders. Between 1886 and 1889 seven trade unions were formed in Sweden and, with one exception, they were all composed of skilled workers; the compositors, the painters, the iron and metal workers, the shoe workers, the woodworkers, and the tailors. The exception was the Postmen's Union.

As the trade unions grew in strength, they took on an ideology, a bolder coloration. The strong current of nineteenth-century socialism made itself felt in the north of Europe. It offered a formula as clearly defined, as nicely delineated, as the concept of the *laissez faire* economists and, naturally, it appealed to men who knew the full horror of "the system," capitalism. There was a direction, a motive, a new and powerful impulse.

This was the second stage in trade-union development. Here were no naïve efforts at self-defense. The trade unions had formed central federations, national in scope, intended to focus the power of labor and the accrued force of union activity. What is more the movement took on an international character with the first Scandinavian labor conference ever held, in Gothenburg in 1886. And this conference made a statement of labor's objectives that was remarkable for its clarity and force:

Politically our object shall be to influence legislation to the end that workers may achieve political equality and thereby prevent capitalist exploitation. For this reason the trade unions ought to deal with all matters of interest to the workers, whether they be of an economic or political nature. We recognize that private capitalist exploitation prevents the attainment of happiness and satisfaction in society and subscribe therefore to the principles of socialism.

Our primary economic objective shall be to secure wage scales acceptable to workers and employers. The conference declares in favor of an hourly wage as opposed to piecework. It recommends the establishment of benefit funds, which may be of importance during strikes and illness. The conference further recommends the creation of unemployment funds.

The conference calls for centralization of the trade-union movement and, owing to the increasing use of machinery, demands the introduction of the eight-hour day. The establishment of arbitration courts for the settlement of industrial disputes between workers and employers is recommended and it is urged that no strike be declared until every peaceful method has been tried and failed. The conference calls for the organization of agricultural workers who are drifting to the towns and by their low wages threatening the standards of urban workers. The conference agrees to agitate for the introduction of universal suffrage and expresses its gratification at the organization of employers as by this means it becomes easier to conduct wage negotiations and the chances of a satisfactory settlement are greatly increased.

For the times this was a remarkable document, and particularly that last clause approving the organization of employers. While there was more and more emphasis on the political and the doctrinaire, this was largely on the surface. It was, after all, during the 'nineties that the trade unions began to lay the foundation for a practical, routine kind of trade unionism of the British type. Even though union leaders took an active part in the fight for suffrage and carried out a general political strike, in 1902, they kept the politicians in their place and were acutely aware of the danger of neglecting the practical work of trade unionism.

In 1898 the Swedish trade-union congress that established the National Trade-Union Federation adopted a resolution declaring that any trade union or association of trade unions wishing to join the federation must affiliate with the Social-Democratic party within three years after admission. This stirred such an angry storm of protest in the newspapers and within the trade unions themselves that the bylaw was never enforced and two years later it was repealed. Many trade-union members believed in strict political neutrality, they were opposed even to the general declaration, subsequently adopted, that the National Federation should work to bring about the affiliation of all local trade-union branches to the local Labor party organization. In spite of opposition, however, this was allowed to stand in the preamble to the federation's rules.

In the first years of the present century there were in Sweden a number of bitter, long-drawn-out strikes and from these conflicts the workers emerged with no small degree of success. Labor felt its power. In 1905 the mere threat of a general strike swung the balance for peace in the bitter dispute over Norway's demand for independence from Sweden. Influenced by Syndicalist doctrine imported from the continent, the leaders believed that the general strike was the instrument with which to bring about the ultimate conquest of power, the end of capitalist exploitation, the beginning of socialism.

Employers were frightened. In order to meet the fierce attacks directed at individual companies by the growing trade-union movement an organization of employers was started shortly after the turn of the century. There was a growing determination to put down trade unionism before it should become any more powerful. Every time the unions made a demand, they got a lockout in response, as in 1903 when nine molders asked for an increase in pay and the employers locked out nearly 9,000 metal workers.

The issue was forced in 1909. Certain employers declared a lockout and labor's answer was a general strike. It was a form of civil war, a war of attrition in which labor held strictly to lawful means. No one had foreseen just what this would mean, the swift depletion of union resources, the tightening of belts, the weeks and months stretching out painfully. And the other side had money, prestige, the brass-hatted military, a press that functioned after a fashion even though printers were out, and above all, the solid support of the middle class. What had seemed a short, inevitable road to power began to look very like a dead end. The general strike was a disastrous failure and defeated men crept back to work, hoping only that their names were not on the long black lists that almost every employer drew up. It was the end of the second phase of labor's rise.

Any attempt to summarize the period that followed is certain to make it sound too easy. It is difficult, impossible perhaps, to give any idea of the care, the effort, the devotion, the loyalty, that contributed to the steady growth of the trade unions in the years that followed 1909. Thousands of men and women worked doggedly, unceasingly, for the movement. They taught study circles, they wrote propaganda, they organized local branches and harangued their fellow workers, they ran for public office when it was merely an exercise in political education, they marched in parades and picketed with strikers, they raised funds and kept trade-union books. It is difficult, as I say, to give any idea of the scope of this struggle, to understand it in terms of the thousands of individuals who contributed to it. There was one advantage: employers no longer questioned the right of workers to organize and they accepted, in principle at least, the process of collective bargaining.

In the prosperous years, 1906 and 1907, the trade unions enrolled a total of 186,226 members. The following year enrollment fell off somewhat. After the disaster of 1909 thousands of members resigned, they emigrated to America or they went back to farming. In 1909 the total membership was 85,176, less than half of what it had been two years before. From this low point it has continued ever since to grow. The curve of growth mounts steadily, with here and there in times of great prosperity, as in the period immediately following the war, a sharp upward climb. Today there are more than 800,000 members, nearly one sixth of the whole population; in proportion to size the most powerful trade-union movement in the world as speakers are fond of boasting. And this, it must be remembered, is in a country in which as late as 1920 more than 44 per cent of the people were dependent upon agriculture, fishing, or forestry for a living with only 35 per cent of the population in industry. Comparable figures today show 39.4 per cent rural and 35.7 per cent industrial.

The 800,000 trade-union members belong to 41 separate unions which are affiliated to the National Federation. While this compares with more than a thousand separate unions in Great Britain and signifies a high degree of industrial unionism, Swedish trade unionists are nevertheless very familiar with the craft-industrial conflict. For more than forty years leaders have sought to establish the movement on an industrial basis, realizing that the old craft forms place a serious handicap on labor organization in a world of machines. They have met with the stubborn resistance of craftsmen determined to maintain higher rates of pay and the other real or imaginary privileges of the "aristocracy of labor."

As early as 1890 consolidations were taking place, breaking down old craft boundaries. Where the craft point of view persisted most strongly unskilled workers were compelled to form unions of their own, even when they worked side by side with skilled craftsmen. It was in this year that unskilled labor formed the organization which was subsequently to become the General Factory Workers' Union. Industrial unions like that formed by the metal workers were still the exception rather than the rule. The Iron and Metal Workers' Union included not only molders and steel workers, but men in the building trades, electricians, and plumbers, a whole series of crafts, goldsmiths, silversmiths, and ordinary blacksmiths. Later the molders and the electricians were to break away and establish their own unions.

The National Federation drew up a plan intended to develop industrial unions in 1912. It was remarkable enough that the subject should have come up for discussion at all at this early date but that a plan favoring the industrial form should have been adopted is nothing short of extraordinary. The federation congress was a little timid and the proposal was somewhat lost sight of in succeeding years. Nevertheless the fact remains that such a design for future development was prepared more than twenty-five years ago.

From time to time there were consolidations. Separate unions of bakers, stokers, gloveworkers, hatters, glassworkers, ropemakers, seafaring women, leatherworkers, corkworkers, butchers and meat packers, cake and pastry makers, tramway employees, coopers, tailors, and furworkers all have been eliminated in the gradual process of industrialization.

Yet the trade-union congress of 1926 agreed that it was necessary to accelerate this process greatly and therefore adopted a plan of reorganization which, when carried out, would leave only 33 unions. In the ten years that have passed but slight progress has been made toward the final goal and the reason is the stubborn resistance of the building trades. As in almost every other industrialized nation, the craft monopoly represented in the building-trade unions in Sweden has stood in the way of the realization of a really functional, that is to say, an industrial, trade-union movement. And, as will be seen, this entrenched and persistent monopoly has hampered the whole social policy of the labor government.

The number of trade unions in 1929 was 44. Consolidation of leather, rubber, and chemical workers reduced this number. And included in the present-day total, 41, are certain small unions which exist chiefly out of a kind of traditionalism. One such union is that of the chimney sweeps with 529 members, and another is the tileworkers with 493. The real objective of the 1926 plan was to bring all building workers together in one big union; that is, to consolidate the three largest single unions in the building trade—the carpenters, the general building workers, and the bricklayers. Later other unions were to be brought in, electricians, painters, roofers, and stoneworkers and at a still later stage this consolidated union was to be combined with the separate union of canal and road builders.

In most of the unions involved referenda were taken, with union leaders favoring the plan of consolidation. The carpenters and the general building workers voted "yes" but the bricklayers turned the plan down. And that, for the time being at least, meant an end to hopes for consolidation, particularly when later the roofers, painters, and stoneworkers followed the lead of the bricklayers. Plumbers and steel constructors now belong to the industrial union that includes all metal workers and so they were not involved. All this does not mean that any serious antagonism exists either between the craft unions and those organized on the vertical, industrial basis or among the separate unions in the building trade. There is in fact a high degree of coöperation among the building groups.

For the purpose of reaching basic national wage agreements the workers in the building trades, including tinners and roofers, carpenters, electricians, unskilled workers, bricklayers, painters, stoneworkers, and transport workers, have combined in an association or cartel. And in addition in many communities there are local cartels of these same workers, a united front for bargaining over details of local wage agreements. In other industries there are similar cartels, notably in the printing trades in which the typographical unions, the lithographers and allied workers, and the bookbinders have formed an association that serves, besides collective bargaining, a variety of common purposes.

While this is a practical working arrangement, it is not industrial unionism. Federation leaders and the heads of individual unions who had urged consolidation did not attempt to conceal their disappointment over the setback to their plans. The trade-union congress that met in 1936 proposed another plan for industrial unionism involving the breakup of a number of small unions. The rubber workers and the chemical workers were to go into the General Factory Workers' Union; the industrial leather workers were to go with the Shoe and Leather Workers' Union. What is more, the congress agreed that the representative assembly, an executive council which meets annually, should have power to compel a referendum of members of the unions involved. That is, the assembly might go so far as to refuse affiliation with the federation to any union refusing to take a referendum of its membership. This drastic power has not yet been invoked. But the action of the congress indicates plainly the determination of trade-union leaders to force a showdown on the industrial issue.

Leaders in the building trades are sensitive to the criticism directed at their unions for failure to yield. In a graph of the wage structure the hourly rate of bricklayers and carpenters is a peak that looms far above the average level. What this means in relation to the problem of housing and the policies of the Social-Democratic government will be shown in a later chapter. In more ways than one the craft unions in the building industry have embarrassed Laborites attempting to follow new economic and social paths.

Besides the craft unions within the federation, there are a few with negligible membership, less than 25,000, outside the central organization. Such a union is that of the locomotive engineers, outside the general Railway Men's Union, and another is the Union of Customshouse Workers. Negotiations are now in progress to bring the former within the federation fold. Still another group of organized workers, also very small, is outside the central body. These are the Syndicalist trade unions and their history and recent rapid decline make a revealing chapter in Swedish labor history.

An outgrowth of the general strike of 1909 and the Syndicalist convictions of a minority within the federation, these unions have in recent years had their greatest strength in the building trades, with lesser fractions among the miners and the metal workers. Altogether the Syndicalist movement enrolls less than 5 per cent of the trade-union movement. Except in isolated instances—small mines or industries—the Syndicalist unions have been a minor voice and therefore they have played a relatively small part in collective bargaining and in the labor movement. Nevertheless they have been an aggressive political fraction.

There was a move in 1929 to merge the Syndicalist unions with those within the federation. It involved the personal fortunes of one of the most dramatic figures in recent labor history, Edvard Mattson, the present head of the Miners' Union. A Syndicalist at the beginning of his career, Mattson clung to his convictions after the general strike of 1909. Known as a radical, on the black lists of Swedish employers, he came to America not long after the big strike had failed. In his career as a casual laborer, first in the Middle West, Minnesota, and Wisconsin, he always maintained union affiliations, allying himself with the group that dominated the trade at which he happened to be working. During this period he belonged to at least two unions within the American Federation of Labor.

Later this adventurous Swede made his way to Alaska and took part, unsuccessfully, in more than one gold rush. Drifting back to Seattle, he discovered the I.W.W. Active in the movement at the time was a friend he had known in Chicago, "Big Bill" Haywood. He admired Haywood, he remembers him today as a brilliant man, an impassioned idealist. And he found in the Wobbly movement a fire, an aggressiveness, the hope of large things to be attained through the solidarity of the working class, not unlike that which had activated the leaders in Sweden's general strike. This was at a time when professional patriots in America, using the war as their justification, were engaged in a campaign to destroy the I.W.W. by any means whatsoever. Mattson was with the Wobblies who challenged the right of the authorities of Everett, Washington, to forbid a union demonstration. The demonstrators chartered a boat at Seattle to go to Everett, intending to parade through the town. But as they neared the dock, there was a burst of gunfire and a number of the men who crowded the forward deck were either killed or seriously wounded. With the dead and dying on board, the boat, at the order of the leaders of the ill-fated expedition, put back to Seattle, there to be met by deputy sheriffs who arrested virtually all the survivors. Miraculously, for he had been with those on the prow of the boat, Mattson escaped injury and somehow, too, he escaped arrest.

This was the violent end of his participation in the American labor movement. Returning to Sweden, he soon became active again in his old union, the Syndicalist Miners, which at that time still had considerable strength, although, of course, nothing approaching a majority, at Grängesberg, Kiruna, and the other big mining towns in the north. From his start as an organizer Mattson rose rapidly to a position of leadership, and in 1929 was named to a committee composed on the one hand of representatives of Syndicalist unions and on the other of representatives of federation unions. The committee was instructed to find some way to merge the two organizations peacefully.

There were five Syndicalist representatives and five federation representatives and the prospect of unification seemed excellent as they met. After an exchange of views and long and thorough discussion a plan of consolidation was put forward and on the first ballot the five federation representatives and four of the Syndicalist delegates voted in favor of it. The lone member in opposition was Albert Jensen, editor of *Arbetaren,* the daily newspaper of the Syndicalists. Jensen proceeded to use the paper as his personal forum, writing almost daily diatribes against the proposed consolidation. His campaign was so effective that when the issue came before the congress of the Syndicalist trade unions that year a majority rejected the proposal. With this Mattson took the floor and in a dramatic speech declared the vote was a tragic mistake, "a crime against the working class." He insisted that since all but one member of the committee had approved the plan, it was up to the congress to adopt it. He declared his intention of resigning from the Miners' Union in which the Syndicalists had their chief strength. And the other three Syndicalists who had voted with him on the committee followed his lead.

At the same time the Miners' Union within the federation was holding its congress. The president who had held office for many years was retiring. To succeed him the convention named Mattson and a delegation was sent to the hall where the Syndicalists were meeting to ask him to accept. All his past, his loyalties, his beliefs, were involved in the decision he had to make. He accepted the offer, knowing that he would promptly be accused of "selling out," which was, of course, what happened.

A number of miners left the Syndicalist union at this time and the decline of the Syndicalist labor movement has been even more rapid in recent years. At each succeeding congress Mattson has been reëlected president of the Miners' Union affiliated with the federation. He says he is now convinced that a policy of reform, based on the political power of a strongly organized trade-union movement, is the only practical way to advance the working class.

Tall and strongly built with a big, serious face, Mattson directs the affairs of his union from headquarters at Grängesberg. These offices have an air of order and efficiency in accord with the bearing of the man who sits at the broad desk in the inner room. As in most trade unions in Scandinavia, strict discipline is maintained in the miners' organization. One rule forbids local branches employing union funds to subsidize political papers. Communists gained control of the locals at Kiruna, Malmberget, and one or two other mining centers. They appropriated union funds for a Communist paper. As a result, 1,400 members were expelled and they were not taken back into the union until they had signed a pledge of loyalty.

Stern measures are taken, too, against nonunion workers who dare to violate picket lines. The names of strikebreakers are printed in the labor press. Their "proven" offenses are cited and until recently they were followed by the phrase, "and may be treated accordingly." Now, under a new interpretation of labor law, this latter prescription is not allowed. But in a strong union community the implied permission is superfluous. The crime itself carries a bitter stigma. In a small town it may mean complete ostracism, the face of every man turned away from the traitor. As will be seen in a later chapter, the trade unions prosecute strikes, blockades, and boycotts with a grim and unrelenting determination.

There is a kind of discipline that has been effective even though it has not been sanctioned by the bylaws of the unions. The Swedish worker moves at a deliberate tempo and he is deeply resentful of devices intended to speed up production, the stretch-out in its various forms. Numerous wage scales are fixed on a piecework basis in Sweden and the tendency is, of course, to fix the rate on the basis of the performance of the fastest workers. This penalizes those who are less efficient and it may, even within the limits set by the formal wage agreement between company and union, work a serious hardship on numerous employees. Therefore the local union in shops or mines where the tempo is exaggerated checks up rather carefully on workers who exceed the average pace. And these workers are assessed—fined—by their local union an amount, that, by a curious coincidence, is equal to the extra pay they made when they exceeded the average rate of production. It should be added that such instances of informal discipline are rare. In certain trades, notably in building where piecework rates are high, the output per man is also high.

Swedish trade unions are among the wealthiest in the world. Through the years they have built up a large per capita wealth. There is today on deposit in Swedish banks more than $15,-000 of union funds.* Another $2,500,000 of union wealth is invested in a variety of ways. Virtually all unions have for many years had their own unemployment funds out of which they have cared for their own members who were without work. In the period from 1899 to 1935 the unions paid out nearly $17,-000,000 in unemployment benefits. It was because of this trade-union system of unemployment relief that the government delayed so long in adopting a system of state unemployment insurance. The measure did not come until 1934. Similarly the

* All figures presented in dollars are arrived at by transposing the Swedish krona at its face value, 25 cents. This is not a true measure of real value, purchasing power, however. There are economists who believe that the krona is worth more nearly 50 cents in purchasing power than 25 cents.

unions have their own employment exchanges and the Ministry of Social Affairs does not include in its public unemployment figures trade-union members who are out of work but still receiving union benefits.

The trade unions in Scandinavia have so firmly established their responsibility that they are entrusted with important functions of government, particularly those relating to labor. In Denmark the entire system of unemployment insurance is built around the unions. All trade-union members are required to contribute to the unemployment fund maintained by the group to which they belong. Under this system there are today nearly 400,000 insured workers, virtually all union members. To come under this insurance system it is almost essential, as it works out practically, to belong to a union and the number of insured persons who are not trade unionists is therefore negligible. Of the 70 unemployment funds approved by the state, 68 are restricted to certain trades but cover the entire country, one is local in character, and one is not restricted to either trade or locality.

Both the Danish state and the commune contribute to the unemployment fund, the state providing two thirds of the public contribution, the commune one third. Because they are managed by the unions, along with other trade-union activities, the funds are administered with remarkable economy. This system was first established in 1907. During the crisis of unemployment that occurred after 1920 it was necessary to supplement the system with a program of public works and to finance this, a State Unemployment Fund was created. In 1933 a new act was passed providing for the establishment of special "crisis funds" within the unemployment funds administered by the unions, the state and commune to contribute in larger proportion for this purpose, and with supplementary aid from a State Unemployment Fund. The latter is created by the contributions of employers who must pay slightly more than $1 a year for each worker who is employed for a certain number of weeks in the year. The State Unemployment Fund is administered by a committee made up of representatives of employers and employees.

The dues paid by union members vary widely in amount, depending upon the income of the membership. Compositors in Sweden paid $31 in 1935, the largest individual contribution made to any union. The regular annual dues in the painters' union are $26. Lithographers pay $24 a year. But postmen pay only $6, and members of the Union of Mental Hospital Staffs slightly more than $4. The latter are government employees and their civil service salaries are not high. For special income groups, for women, and for minors there are in some instances special rates. The entrance dues to most unions in Sweden are exceptionally low. In the Metal Workers' Union, with its 150,-000 members representing nearly one fifth of the whole trade-union movement, entrance dues are only three kronor for a full-paying member.

The salaries paid to union officials are in accord with the modest scale of contributions. None of the 400 full-time officials paid to carry on the work of the Trade-Union Center, that is, the central offices of the federation in Stockholm, or the national unions, receives more than $2,000 a year. With one possible exception these officers are all of working-class origin. Almost without exception they are self-educated and many of them are well educated. Sigfrid Hansson, a former bricklayer, has made himself a recognized authority on the history of the labor movement. Some years ago he was given the degree of Doctor of Philosophy by the University of Stockholm, an honor not lightly passed about, for his contribution to knowledge in the field of labor. Until recently he has been head of the trade-union educational movement.

The president of the federation—*Lands-Organisationen* known as L.O.—is August Lindberg, a former sawmill worker. In many respects he is typical of the present generation of trade-union leaders. They are keenly aware of the need to shape a new and broader policy, freed of the old traditionalism and the deadening blight of bureaucracy. They realize that if the trade-union movement is to expand and grow, if it is not to suffer the fate that has overwhelmed it elsewhere, the entire economy of the country must be considered in relation to labor's policy and not merely one narrowly defined class. They approach present-day problems with a sense of their grave responsibility for a common solution, an earnest intelligence that not infrequently rises above partisanship.

A new wage policy is being formulated as a result of action

taken by the last trade-union congress which met in 1936. Many speakers at that congress pointed to the urgent need for raising wage levels of the lowest paid workers even though this might mean that the highest paid workers would have to make a temporary sacrifice. The position of agricultural laborers and the workers in the forests was particularly stressed. Albert Forslund, who was retiring as president to become Minister of Transportation in the Labor-Farmer cabinet, in his opening address called attention to the way in which farmers and industrial workers had begun to collaborate politically in recent years and to the collaboration that is growing up between manual workers and salaried employees in both state and private service.

He said:

The workers form an important element in the community, and the trade-union movement is one of the instruments for the realization of their legitimate demands. However, we cannot leave out of consideration the fact that we are a part of the community. We must direct our activities in such a way that our efforts may be to the advantage of the whole and not of one group alone.

The move for a new and broader wage policy was linked with the objective of shared social control over the management of industry, expressed in a resolution submitted to the congress by the Metal Workers' Union. The increased influence that the trade-union movement has achieved, this resolution declared, must be accompanied by greater responsibility for the welfare of the whole of society. Labor must collaborate to develop and strengthen the nation's industries in a sound and rational way and, in order to do this, the trade unions must obtain for all workers some authority over the management of industry. This and other similar motions were approved by the congress and it was agreed to refer the problem to a special committee empowered to call upon economic experts and consult with members of the government and committees of Parliament.

Announcing the appointment of a committee of fifteen not long afterward, August Lindberg made a highly significant speech. It was possible, he said, to raise the wage level of agricultural labor by means of government subsidies to farmers, but any substantial increase in industrial wages could come only through an increase in efficiency. To this end, labor could contribute materially. But if the workers were to coöperate, then they must be guaranteed a more secure place in the economic structure. They had political power, they could determine, within limits, the conditions of labor and hours of work. But before the ultimate right of the employer to hire and fire they were helpless. It was all very well to talk about the worker's equal right to leave his job. That was merely theoretical since the employer's power of ownership of the means of production placed him in an altogether superior position. In the management of industry labor now had no voice whatsoever. Uncertainty and fear had become intolerable during the widespread unemployment that prevailed during the depression. The new committee had been formed to shape a plan for the solution of these major problems and what was more the members had been impressed with the urgency of their task.

The wisdom of this approach is obvious. Labor declares its willingness to participate in a drive to raise the level of industrial production at the same time that it points to the anomalous position of the worker; his complete dependence upon industry, the inherent limitations of the power of even his most highly developed organizations, his fear and uncertainty in the face of the economic cycle. The recommendations of the committee will undoubtedly be a factor of primary importance in determining future policies of the trade-union movement.

No one pretends that in arriving at decisions of such far-reaching significance there is unbroken harmony within the ranks of organized labor. This would be on its face impossible and not to be desired even if it were possible. There is in fact a perceptible division between Left and Right that follows roughly the line of age. The older trade-union leaders tend to be more conservative than the younger rank and file, more cautious and discreet than the younger men who are now coming into positions of leadership. It is natural that this should be so. The older men have been concerned with the minutiae of collective bargaining. A victory involving six kronor a week looms very large when one has been engaged for many years in a specific and restricted field.

To a certain degree they have imbibed the point of view of

the representatives of industry whom they have faced across so many conference tables. They have come to doubt the possibility of revolutionary change, these older and more conservative leaders. The discipline of present-day industry is a harsh one; it must be modified in many ways. The margin dividing the rich, or merely the well-off, from the poor is wide; it must be greatly narrowed. But what effective discipline will you substitute for the present industrial discipline, they demand of the rising generation. And can you provide a more efficacious means for distributing the products of the machine than the competitive system? When management performs a genuine function, then management is entitled to a fair share of the profits, these older leaders hold. They are inclined to differentiate between "working capitalists" and capitalists who live off unearned income. In support of their point of view is the upward curve of wages, a real gain of 50 per cent in a comparatively short period.

The younger men listen to the reasoning of their elders but they remain somewhat skeptical. They fear that the division between Right and Left is likely to become sharper, that a wave of Fascism sweeping across Europe may inspire extremists on the Right to attempt similar repressive methods for breaking the power of labor in Scandinavia. And for this reason they are more concerned with the revolutionary background and traditions of the labor movement, doubtful of the benevolent face that capital wears in the present interval. It is one of the shrewdest and most observing of these younger men, however, who says that the youth movement is 98.9 per cent loyal to Per Albin and the blue-and-yellow line he has taken.

The division between younger men and women and their elders, insofar as it exists at all, was illustrated by the labor exposition put on by the Social-Democratic youth organization in Stockholm in the fall of 1937. The theme of the exposition, "Organized Labor Has the Word," was written in large white letters on a red flag that blazed across the advertising placards announcing the show. The visitor to Liljevalchs Hall saw the history of the Swedish labor movement done in photo-murals, clever stage sets, emblazoned slogans, with the stress throughout placed upon revolutionary episodes. Here was the general strike of 1909, a photograph of the period enlarged to cover almost an entire wall, grim, brass-helmeted soldiers in an un-broken ring and the scattering, helpless force of the workers. In another room was a photo-mural of a May Day demonstration, men marching proudly with banners in the wind. There was ex-tended treatment in posters and enlarged photographs of the tragedy that occurred in 1931 when striking paper-mill workers in the north were fired upon by troops with several killed and many injured for the first time in Swedish labor history. One display dramatized the weaknesses of the capitalist system with its recurring crises of unemployment. A short motion picture film shown by an automatic projector pointed to living stand-ards much too low.

The older trade-union leaders did not care for this exposition. It placed far too much emphasis, they said, upon isolated epi-sodes of little real importance in labor's rise to power. And the revolutionary philosophy that infused it, they added, was not characteristic of the Swedish trade-union movement. The younger generation found the exposition good. For them it was not radical enough. They objected that the general impact of the display, strong as it was, suffered dilution from the intrusion of exhibits by the Coöperative Union and H.S.B., the largest co-operative housing society. They were inclined to be indignant at finding a display of coöperative bacon and coöperative plumb-ing in the midst of labor's own story. The secret was, of course, that the financial help of H.S.B. and the Coöperative Union was essential to the exposition.

From all this it must not be inferred that there is any active hostility between these so-called Lefts and Rights. It is, rather, that there is a more or less constant pressure from the younger generation, the younger radicals in the trade unions and the So-cial-Democratic party. They want a more aggressive policy, more action. And not infrequently they make their influence felt.

In Denmark the situation is quite a different one although the origins of the trade-union movement are more or less similar, with the basic conflict that assured labor the right to organize coming earlier, in 1899. There has never been a concerted ef-fort in Denmark to rationalize trade-union structure and there-fore a number of small craft unions survive today, affiliated to a complex, bureaucratic central organization. The Danish trade-union movement resembles more nearly the German than the British model and there are critics, particularly on the Left, who see ominous portents in the present trend. They fear the same weaknesses that undermined labor in pre-Hitler Germany may ultimately cause the downfall of Danish labor. It is above all the disease of bureaucracy which obscures reality and makes adjustment to changing circumstances difficult or impossible.

In the classified section of the Copenhagen telephone directory there are more than three pages of small type, three columns to a page, devoted to trade-union organizations. And while these are not all national federations, it is nevertheless a rough measure of the ramifications of the labor bureaucracy. Craft unions of craftsmen who have all but vanished in the modern industrial world still survive. There is a union of gilders with 170 members; glaziers with 180 and glassworkers with 424. The Cork Cutter's Union has 195 members, coppersmiths 254, coopers 417, pavers 280, divers 63. Those are extreme samples but they illustrate how the trade-union membership of this small country—the total in the central organization is nearly 430,000—is split up.

Then, too, curious anomalies and inconsistencies exist within this complex organization. Women form a part of the membership of most unions, with the largest number, 12,000, in the Union of Textile Workers, and only slightly less, 10,000, in the Garment Workers' Union. But there is also a separate general union for women in industry with a membership of nearly 19,-000. The difficulties and confusion that arise as a result of this overlapping of organization, particularly with relation to collective bargaining, are not hard to imagine. Moreover, the inevitable duplication and the very excess of organization put a needless charge upon labor. To offset these obvious disadvantages cartels have been formed by unions that have certain interests in common. For example, eight organizations made up of metal workers have through a cartel established a joint leadership, a joint unemployment fund, and a common union journal. Twenty-one organizations of civil servants have formed a cartel for similar purposes as have also nine unions made up of vari-

ous types of workers in the wood industry. In that this is a recognition of the need for consolidation, it is at least a beginning.

Again in contrast to the practice in Sweden, there is in Denmark not even a nominal separation between the trade unions
and the Social-Democratic party. The propaganda center, known
as H.I.P.A. from the initials of the four long words that make
up its title, *Hovedorganisationernes Informations og Propa-
ganda-afdeling,* functions for both the trade unions and the Socialist party and to its support members of the party and the
union must make small contributions. H.I.P.A. directs all
workers' education, including special courses for both trade-
union and political leaders. From the offices of H.I.P.A. there is
issued monthly a printed bulletin that contains information on
current social and economic problems. Formerly it went only to
leaders of the 1,300 sections that comprise the Socialist party in
Denmark but now it goes also to 7,000 trade-union officials. This
bulletin, *Socialdemokratiske Noter,* is in a sense ammunition to
be used in labor's unceasing campaign for a larger share of the
national income. Also H.I.P.A. publishes *Red Youth,* the journal of the Danish Socialist youth organization. And this is only
to list a few of the numerous activities that are centered in two
floors of a Copenhagen office building.

There is a high degree of organization; perhaps, as I have
suggested, overorganization. Breweries play a part in the cultural life of Denmark that is unique, with the great Tuborg
and Carlsberg brewing firms turning over a large proportion of
their profits to endow museums and philanthropic institutions.
So it is not surprising to learn that labor has its own brewery and
its own trademark, The Star, ranking next in production after
the two great private firms. Labor's Star Brewery was started in
1902 with funds supplied from the surplus capital accumulated
by a bakery owned coöperatively by the trade unions and by individual subscriptions. It has grown into an enterprise of no
little importance, selling fifty million bottles of beer and mineral water in 1935, with an annual turnover of more than a
quarter of a million dollars. The Star Brewery got its real start
in 1919 when there was a strike against Tuborg and Carlsberg
and loyal Laborites had perforce to switch over to their own

beer. The Star quality has steadily improved until today many connoisseurs insist that the lager produced by the trade-union brewery is superior to all other lagers.

From temperance and prohibition sources within the labor movement has come opposition to this industry. To offset the criticism of prohibitionists the Star Brewery has developed a beer of low alcoholic content that is also very potable. In its advertising and propaganda the management of the Star Brewery tries to push this temperance beer and nonalcoholic beverages which are also produced. What is more, a fund is set aside out of the profits for workers' education. A fairly large sum has accumulated and it is now proposed to spend this for a building which will be the center of the workers' education movement in the country.

The demand for free beer from loyal trade unionists has never been a problem since long ago rules were established strictly limiting this privilege. Unemployed members of trade unions may visit their brewery at least once a year and drink all the beer they can hold. The brew and malt houses, all done in the finest brewery architecture, cover a considerable area. It is an impressive sight and no less so is Director Svendsen, a former trade-union official, who sports a generous sweep of handle-bar moustache and a smile befitting such a post.

This is, of course, only one small incidental element in the complex structure of Danish trade unionism. Out of this very complexity problems have come. It will be seen in a later chapter that Danish trade-union leaders are today faced with the necessity for making grave decisions regarding the use of the strike as a weapon in collective bargaining and the degree to which individual unions can be allowed to retain their autonomy in wage negotiations.

In Norway the whole cycle of the labor movement is in a much earlier phase because industries were later in developing there than in Denmark and Sweden. Norwegian industry is in fact still largely owned abroad and Laborites now in power are making a serious effort to encourage home industries. Most industrial workers in Norway are not very many years removed from the land. Their fathers or perhaps they themselves knew the independence of a small holding, and they have not been

slow to show their resentment of the regimen of modern industry, particularly in its more grim phases. This has made for a
trade-union movement with a strong revolutionary undercurrent.
More radical at one period than almost any other labor movement in the world, Norwegian labor after the Russian revolution left the International Federation of Trade Unions to join
the Red International under the guardianship of Moscow.

Gradually, as the political history of the past fifteen years
will show, labor has been retreating from this extreme position.
But within the rank and file there is nevertheless a strong in-
heritance of revolutionary ardor which expresses itself in the
form of impatience with leaders who are trying to carry out
moderate policies. Today there are about a quarter of a million
organized workers in thirty-three national unions.

The closest coöperation exists between the trade unions of
the Scandinavian countries as well as between the Socialist parties that now govern all three. Each year a conference is held in
one of the capitals attended by representatives of the central
trade-union federations and the Social-Democratic parties. Usually the president of the federation attends the conference and
one or more government officials, sometimes a cabinet officer.
At the conference held in Stockholm in 1937 the Prime Minister of Sweden, Per Albin Hansson, presided, and the delegates
included Norway's Minister of Social Affairs, Oscar Torp, and
Finland's Minister of Finance, Väinö Tanner. Finland and Ice-
land as well as Norway, Sweden, and Denmark are represented
at these yearly conferences.

Questions of common interest are brought up, the 40-hour
week, unemployment, the cost of living in relation to wage
agreements, and discussed freely and fully. The conference may
adopt resolutions embodying the view of Scandinavian labor on
important issues, a common front that is, to say the least, impressive. It is an opportunity, too, to discuss in private the problems that confront labor in each of these countries, to exchange
information and ideas.

At the last congress of the Swedish trade-union movement in
Stockholm it was proposed to carry this collaboration a step
further. In his inaugural address August Lindberg suggested
that it might be possible to work out an arrangement whereby

the Scandinavian countries could exchange workers in various fields. His idea was that Danish workers might go to Norway to work for three to six months at the same time that Norwegian workers went to Denmark. Understanding and coöperation would be promoted among the rank and file through such a practical exchange of experience.

It is a long way from the little man at the bottom to these men at the top who are charged with so great a responsibility, leading nearly a million and a half workers in a period of grave uncertainty. But the little man has a voice and a vote and he may go as far as his energy and capacity will take him in the movement that is his own. This is a democracy, labor's own democracy, directed by men from the ranks.

CHAPTER II

HOW INDUSTRY HAS ORGANIZED

IF labor has organized, so has industry and perhaps even more cohesively. While the employers' associations that have developed in the three Scandinavian countries do not cover so large a proportion of industry as the trade unions, they are able to pool the resources of their members in such a way as to present an unbroken front in the face of labor strife. But their function is primarily a peaceful one; that is to carry out collective bargaining in the major industries.

Employers in Scandinavia long ago recognized the right of labor to organize. In fact it was in response to the growing power of organized labor that these associations of employers came into being. That at any rate is the explanation given in the official literature of the employer associations. In Scandinavia it would be difficult to find a responsible large-scale employer who would make any fundamental change in the orderly system of collective bargaining that exists today. As will be seen later, the basic objections come from labor's side. Many employers say that they find it easier to deal with one big union. It is not a question of a choice between the system that exists today and what preceded it, the confusion and uncertainty inevitable in a completely unorganized labor market. No one would return to the past.

This is not to say that employers in Scandinavia are in accord with labor's point of view. On the contrary, the employer associations are thoroughly hardboiled, resisting wage increases each step of the way and yielding only when the overwhelming weight of public opinion appears to be on labor's side. But the important thing to observe is that there is a method carefully worked out for carrying on wage disputes. It is not simply the law of the jungle. And employers and employees come nearer to discussing their mutual problems in an atmosphere of tolerance and understanding than in any other part of the world that I know of. In recent years they have taken up together around a conference table not only the details of collective bargaining but the broader implications of the relationship between labor, industry, and the state. The fact is that trade unions usually try to force unorganized employers to join the Employers' Association in the hope of getting a more orderly form of bargaining. This is done by demanding higher wages than the national agreement provides; in self-defense the employer must join the association.

More than 4,000 employers who have on their pay rolls nearly 400,000 workers belong to the Swedish Employers' Association. Most major industrial groups, with the exception of the private railways, shipowners, and agricultural employers, are included in the association which devotes itself exclusively to employer-employee relationships. A great many of the industrialists who belong to the association are also members of the Federation of Swedish Industries which is concerned with broader questions, tariffs, taxation, and trade treaties. The fact that the Employers' Association is occupied solely with the problems of employment is undoubtedly an advantage.

Like the central organization of the trade unions, the Employers' Association is made up of a number of federations, each covering a special branch of industry and each equipped to cope with the details of collective bargaining in that branch. Each separate federation has its own paid managing director, its own administrative staff, and its own offices, and to the directors a great deal of authority and responsibility has been delegated. The same is true of the paid directors of the association itself, headed by Gustaf Söderlund. With a long background of experience in the field of collective bargaining, Söderlund has made himself extremely influential, gaining the confidence of trade-union leaders and seeking a more secure and permanent basis for industrial peace.

While the federations that comprise the association have some degree of autonomy, all basic questions relating to wage agreements and wage policies must be referred to a central board made up of fifteen members. No employer or trade federation may make any collective agreement without the approval of this board. A lockout may not be declared by a federation or by an individual employer without the board's approval. And it is up to the board to decide how employer-members of the association who have suffered financial loss from strikes or lockouts shall be compensated. Paragraph 23 of the constitution of the association pledges all members to adhere to these stipulations in the following unmistakable language:

Should a member of the association, or one of its federations wish to enter into a collective agreement with a trade union or a federation of trade unions or any other labor organization, the proposed agreement must be submitted to the board of the association, and no such agreement shall be made without the approval of the board. The board shall also, after consultation with the section or local industrial federation concerned, issue instructions on the application of such collective agreement or on working conditions not regulated by the agreement.

Collective agreements between a member of the association or one of its sectional federations and a trade union shall include a stipulation to the effect that the employer shall have the right to engage and dismiss workers at his discretion, to direct and distribute the work and to employ workers belonging to any union or workers who belong to no union.

An employer who has joined the association is forbidden during a strike or lockout to provide work, directly or indirectly, contrary to the decision of the board, for any striker or locked-out worker, or for any worker otherwise concerned in the dispute, or to assist him in any other way; and the board shall take such action as may be considered necessary to enforce compliance with this rule.

Any member offending against or evading any of the stipulations of this paragraph, or any instructions given on the basis thereof, shall, if his offence was intentional, be held liable for damages.

From this one may gather that the members of the Employers' Association are not sentimentalists. The open-shop stipulation has never particularly disturbed trade unionists. In general trade-union policy in Sweden has been opposed to both the closed shop and the check-off as they are known in America. The feeling has been that a closed shop enforced by a wage agreement is of no real value anyway; it may compel men to join the union but it does not create trade unionists. The view has been held that it is the task of leaders and organizers to bring all workers into the union, by argument, by persuasion, and even by coercion; and, as I tried to show in the last chapter, they have done a very good job of it. The check-off, under which the employer deducts union dues from the pay envelope of the worker, has been opposed for somewhat the same reasons. It has been felt, too, that the check-off puts the employer and the trade union in a relationship that is not altogether desirable.

The basic right of the employer to hire and fire at his own discretion and to direct the work as he chooses has only recently, as was seen in the preceding chapter, been directly challenged. This challenge drew an immediate response from the Employers' Association. In *Industria,* the fortnightly publication of the association, there was an article which sought to show the essential relationship between efficiency in industry and the right of management to hire and fire. To counter the new demands of labor for participation in the direction of industry, said the article, it is unnecessary to speak of the rights of capital or the mobility of capital. It is not even necessary to invoke the rights of ownership. It is sufficient to refer to what is practical. The interference of large masses in the management of a business is an evil, whether it is a mass of workers, a mass of shareholders, a mass of consumers, or a mass of lenders. These influences exist at present to a large extent, but they are always unfortunate, never practical. To yield to such a trend would be to kill efficiency, a crime against the national economy.

All this is very much in character, first of employers in general and more particularly of Swedish employers. It is plain that the Employers' Association will not surrender the right to hire and fire, as guaranteed in Paragraph 23, without a bitter struggle. This may well become the basic issue in the long contest between organized industrialists and organized workers.

As is stipulated in Paragraph 23, members may be, and not infrequently are, fined for violating the bylaws of the association. And there is never any doubt that such fines, or more properly, perhaps, damages, will be collected, for they are determined on the basis of the bond which each member is required to post on assuming membership. This bond, which is never for less than $1,250, serves a double purpose. Besides insuring the collection of damages, it is a source of funds should other income prove insufficient. The size of the bond is determined by the number of workers in an industry, at the rate of $50 for each male worker and $25 for each woman employed.

The Employers' Association has amassed a large war chest. Well over $4,000,000 has been accumulated from the annual subscriptions of members, computed at the rate of $5 for each man employed and $2.50 for each woman. In addition the bonds put up by members represent a capital of nearly $15,000,-000. If no other funds are available, the Committee of Delegates, a supervisory group made up of about forty-five representatives of the federations, can call for payment of these bonds but cannot demand more than 10 per cent of the total amount, at intervals of not less than six months. Members also pay entrance fees and annual subscriptions to their federation, averaging about a quarter of those payable to the association proper.

With the financial backlog built up in this way, the association is prepared to come to the aid of members, or sometimes an entire federation, engaged in a prolonged strike or lockout. After the first eleven days of a conflict, whether it be strike or lockout, an employer is entitled to compensation of 25 cents a day for each worker involved in the dispute. If the conflict lasts longer than three months, this may be doubled. And what is more important, the Committee of Delegates may decide to grant extra compensation in specific cases. This happens fairly frequently. In conflicts where there is a sharp division of issues, a major trial of strength, the delegates sometimes vote large sums.

There is nothing secret about all this. It is perfectly lawful and more or less open for public inspection. The Employers' Association has its offices in Stockholm in a handsome building scarcely a hundred yards from the Grand Hotel and next door to the Automobile Club. Here, too, are the offices of many of the thirty-six federations included in the association, each with its own staff. The association has its own Bureau of Wage Sta-

tistics with a trained personnel. Ordinarily an air of quiet efficiency pervades the association offices. But during the course of
important negotiations or in the event of a major strike it becomes G.H.Q. for industry and lights burn through the night
in a warlike atmosphere.

Largely through the influence of Gustaf Söderlund, representatives of the Employers' Association have come together
with trade-union leaders in an effort to find a common solution
of certain problems that vitally affect these two sides of the industrial triangle. On the third side is the state, representing the
public interest. And it is precisely to avoid ceding to the state a
larger share of authority over industrial relationships than it
now has that labor and industry have come together. At intervals over a period of two years, representatives of the two sides
have met in informal conferences with the common understanding that a way must be found to adjust wage and other differences in more peaceful fashion if the state is not increasingly to
intervene on behalf of the general good.

With government attempting in the face of world confusion
and uncertainty to plan the national economy, prolonged
strikes and lockouts have become a threat to stability that can
scarcely be tolerated. In Denmark compulsory arbitration of
wage disputes, as will be seen in a later chapter, has become in
certain instances not a possibility but a reality. In Sweden both
workers and employers want to avoid compulsory arbitration;
they want to limit the state to its present role of voluntary umpire. What has come out of the informal conferences thus far is
not clear. Apparently nothing of a very tangible nature has been
arrived at as yet. But it is significant that these meetings are
continuing, labor and industry agreeing on the premise that a
more satisfactory method of wage negotiation must be found if
the state is not to step in finally and for all.

Proof of the confidence which trade-union leaders have in
Söderlund is seen in the fact that he is invited each year to come
to the trade-union school at Brunnsvik to explain the employers' point of view in collective bargaining. In these annual lectures he is perfectly frank and straightforward. And the students at the school respond in kind. When he has finished

lecturing, there is a period for questioning and this usually turns into a spirited debate between the rather scholarly, shrewd-looking man on the platform and the alert young trade-union students.

The first lecture that he gave at the school, in June, 1935, has become already a significant document in Swedish labor history. Speaking on the broad theme of "The Conflict between Capital and Labor," the head of the Employers' Association defined the limits to which industry was willing to go in coöperating with the trade unions. Declaring that employers had organized only in response to the organization of labor, he went on to say:

It may be stated here unreservedly that the trade-union movement has achieved a great accomplishment in raising many of the standards of the working class. It has also, with respect to the labor market, created a firm foundation for that instrument of peace and stabilization known as collective bargaining; it has become for the large-scale industries of our time a necessary means of collaboration between employers and workers; it has prepared the way for order. On the other hand it has given the working class ideas and opinions on economic and social questions which must necessarily lead to measures unsound not only for labor but for society as a whole. . . .

Continuing, he cited the tangible gains that unions have achieved for their members. But he pointed also to certain limitations imposed by the force of circumstances on the trade-union movement. In industries producing almost entirely for the home market labor can force wages up and the employer can pass increased costs on to the consumer. In those industries dependent upon the world market, however, the employer cannot pass the cost of wage increases along and therefore he has resisted labor's demands more strenuously. Söderlund expressed, of course, the conservative opinion that wage increases come out of a steady growth of capital and that anything which interferes with the growth of capital interferes likewise with the upward course of wages. It is scarcely necessary to say that he rejected socialism, but he acknowledged that the coöperatives have had a "tremendous success" and through that success have exerted a marked influence on the general price level, while the relationship between coöperative employers and employees has been without serious discord.

No, [he said finally] there is no way to escape the conflict between capital and labor. It is inherent in the very circumstances that exist between them, just as inevitably as the opposition between the seller and the buyer of goods. And the final result is the same even though society be the buyer of the commodity that labor has to offer. But just as the conflict between buyer and seller can be resolved without violence and without lasting bitterness, so should this be possible in the labor market. It is toward this end in my opinion that all effort should be directed instead of toward utopian schemes that seek essentially to conceal the fundamental opposition of interests.

When the trade-union movement appeared with its new strength, it was often not a question of calmly and objectively discussing problems, but simply of beating down one's opponent with a club. This was understandable in the beginning, particularly since employers appeared completely indifferent to the new seekers after power and refused to have any dealings with them. Now both sides have learned a good deal and the troubles of infancy are past. All mutual claims become subject to common deliberation with the objective of reaching a result acceptable to both.

Mutual claims are adjusted for the most part through the process of collective bargaining. It must be acknowledged that the collective agreement has become a stabilizing and pacifying instrument for organized labor. Without such agreements conditions in our country would be exceedingly unstable from the viewpoint of production. Collective agreements create more stable conditions for both sides but they presuppose a well-organized and strong trade-union movement. And the acknowledgment is in order here that Sweden's reformist trade-union movement in this respect comes up to the mark. Industrial peace is guaranteed so long as the agreements are in effect, particularly since the law on collective bargaining and arbitration has given support to the sanctity of agreements. Therefore today it is chiefly in working out new collective agreements that the controversy between capital and labor leads to difficulties which cannot be solved without conflict. The problem is to settle these controversies as peaceably as possible.

I have quoted from this at such length because it seems to me to express so well the point of view of Swedish employers. The cards are all on the table. There is very little breath wasted on propaganda. It is a question of perfectly straightforward bargaining between equals.

The employers' organizations in Norway and Denmark have been developed along essentially these same lines. The General Federation of Danish Employers got an earlier start, the first central organization having been formed in 1896. It has developed slowly and steadily until today it includes virtually all Danish employers. The leadership has shown great resourcefulness in the prolonged and bitter disputes that have occurred in recent years. And while Danish employers were forced to accept nominal defeat, they have succeeded in placing the labor government in a position that may prove embarrassing in the future, as a later chapter will show.

The employer federations of the three countries and that of Finland are all united and each year delegates meet in one of the Scandinavian capitals to discuss common problems. These discussions, which go on for several days, are largely of a practical and technical nature, having to do with the details of collective bargaining. The deliberations of the delegates from the four countries are held behind closed doors and there is no public record of what transpires. Government officials, mediators, and the judges of labor courts frequently attend these annual conventions, reading prepared papers on some special phase of the employer-employee relationship. The experience of one group is passed on for the benefit of another, in just the same way that Scandinavian labor leaders meet each year to talk out their particular problems.

To the outsider it seems that not only employers and workers but everyone in the entire Scandinavian peninsula is organized for the advancement of his or her own interest. Doctors, lawyers, journalists, clerks, shopkeepers, all have come together in one kind of organization or another. And this is not merely joining for the sake of joining. Each group has a practical objective; to get a larger share of the national income, to raise professional standards, to resist the encroachments of the state or competing groups. This part of the world is so completely organized that the individual's life is divided between three or four groups, each essential to some one phase of his existence.

As a consumer he belongs to a coöperative which keeps his household budget in line; as a worker he belongs to a trade union or a professional organization which helps to safeguard his income; as a liberal or a socialist or a conservative he is a member of a political party and participates to some degree in public life.

Despite the extent to which existence is organized, or even, perhaps, because of it, one has a strong sense of the independence of the individual. Whether individual liberties are jeopardized by the power of organized business, organized labor, or organized consumers is a matter for deep and constant concern. No other people in the world today seem so aware of the need not only to protect the ancient rights of man but to reëxamine them realistically in the light of modern practice.

CHAPTER III

BARGAINING FOR WAGES

WITHIN the framework of institutions created by custom and law human beings are inclined to work out their own adjustments and compromises. It is like putting on a new suit of clothes; through usage it will become a part of the wearer, familiar and comfortable. This has been true of the system of collective bargaining that exists in Sweden today. One might put down all the laws and the regulations, ignoring the human shortcuts, the day-to-day practices that have come into being, and there would be missing an essential part of this process of bargaining for wages.

Take a definite example to show how it works. The basic wage agreement in the metal industry is about to expire. It is an important industry for many reasons, employing nearly a hundred thousand workers, many of them highly skilled. Some of the most successful firms in the export field, particularly in steel, are included in this industry. Together with wood pulp the metal industry is the vital core of Swedish economic life. Obviously a great deal depends on its continuing stability.

The present basic wage agreement has been in effect for nearly two years. Under the terms of that agreement—a clause which is included in virtually all wage contracts—the unions must give notice three months in advance of the date of expiration if they are to seek new terms. Unless such notice is given, the old agreement remains in force for an additional year or for such additional time as shall be specified in the contract.

The period during which the agreement has been in force has seen a rapid rise in production. And retail prices have risen above the level of two years ago. Both trade-union leaders and employers are keenly aware of these trends and what they mean with regard to wages in the industry. There is every indication that notice will be given before the last day specified in the contract, October 1.

Well in advance of that date August Lindberg telephones to Gustaf Söderlund to suggest that a preliminary discussion might be a good idea. This, being a major agreement, will, of course, engage the attention of the principals on both sides. So Lindberg goes to Söderlund's office. They have a long and serious discussion. The rank and file in the Metal Workers' Union, Lindberg reports, are not in favor of allowing the old agreement to continue for another year; they feel they are entitled to a wage increase. It will not come easily, Söderlund warns. Manufacturers are faced with a new competitive situation; there is Germany's drive to achieve industrial self-sufficiency. On the desk between them as they talk are indices of production, graphs that show the trend of commodity prices. They cover every phase of the situation before they finish their talk. When they part it is with a mutual understanding of the problems they will confront when negotiations actually begin for a new agreement.

It should be pointed out here, perhaps, that it has been only recently that the federation has taken such active leadership in the matter of wage negotiations. Formerly this devolved almost entirely upon the local union. And still, more often than not, leadership is with the local union. Before the Metal Workers decide upon a course to follow during wage negotiations, a "bargaining conference" is called, at which all locals are represented, to discuss and decide upon the course of action to be taken.

On October 1 the federation and the Metal Workers' Union send formal notices to all parties to the agreement. There are three months in which to negotiate a complex wage scale, covering hundreds of categories of work, hourly rates, piecework rates, working conditions, holidays, overtime, training for apprentices. Once a new agreement containing basic provisions has been negotiated, of course, individual employers may negotiate separate contracts within this framework covering local wage variations and conditions of work. It is a long and difficult task and those who participate in it are prepared to work night and day until it is finally concluded.

The federation has had the assistance of men long familiar with the details of wage negotiation in preparing the case for a

Above: Negotiating a new wage contract in the metal industry; representatives of employers seated at the left and representatives of workers at the right.

Below: Conference of Scandinavian Labor party executives in Stockholm; seated on the platform, from left to right, August Lindberg of the Swedish Trade Union Federation, Prime Minister Per Albin Hansson, Anders Nilsson, secretary of the Social-Democratic party.

general increase that is now presented to the Employers' Association. And the association in turn calls upon expert aid in preparing its reply. Between the two there is a broad difference that represents the trading margin, so broad in the first view that it seems impossible that the two sides can ever come together. The federation has asked for a flat percentage increase covering all wage scales, two weeks' holiday with pay for all workers in the industry, and new overtime provisions that would materially increase the employers' wage bill. It is doubtful, the employers say in their reply, that any addition to labor costs whatever will be possible if the Swedish steel industry is to maintain its competitive world position.

For a week or more conferences continue, with little or no progress. There are some concessions but they are so slight as to leave the gap between the two sides almost as wide as it was in the beginning. An insistent pressure comes from both directions. The rank and file in the trade union are determined to get a tangible advance; it is what they talk about in the meetings of the locals and when they leave the plant. Employers have convinced themselves that any increase will be ruinous. It begins to look as though a new wage agreement were hopelessly remote. There is talk of serious labor trouble after January 1 when the old contract expires. Finally the discussions come to an impasse. Both sides admit defeat. The newspaper headlines report a breakdown of negotiations.

It is at this point that the state mediator, under the terms of the mediation law, enters the situation and immediately begins a new effort to find a basis for mutual agreement. Officially informed on October 1 that notice had been given by the trade union, he does not come into the dispute entirely unaware of what has been happening up to the present time. In fact from the first he has kept closely in touch with the negotiations, offering his advice in a friendly and informal way before he was required by law, with the breakdown of negotiations, to take the initiative. This public mediator is familiar not only with the status of the present disagreement but with the whole background of employment in the industry.

The task of the public mediator now becomes that of a tactician, a diplomatist. Because both sides have confidence in him they tell him what their minimum demands are and it is with the advantage of this knowledge that the mediator confers with first one side and then another. He can hint broadly. If you concede the two weeks' holiday with pay, I think they might be willing to accept a modification on the claim for overtime. And similarly he suggests to trade-union representatives that if they surrender on one or two points, it may be possible to strike a bargain.

But this is a stubborn conflict. There is no yielding on either side. The mediator becomes convinced that neither side has been quite frank in stating minimum demands; they are still determined to obtain the maximum, or nearly the maximum. Nevertheless he cannot go behind what he has been told. It is drawing very close to January 1 and he makes a final effort to persuade the two sides to modify their demands, but without success. On December 24 representatives of the federation give notice of strike. The law requires that this notice be given seven days before a strike is actually called. What the union is saying to the employers and the mediator with this formal notice is, in effect, give us a wage contract we can accept, with more than you have been willing to concede up to the present, inside a week or we will go out on strike.

It is an extremely serious situation, the threat of a stoppage throughout a major industry. In such instances the law provides for a special commission of arbitration. Invariably included on this commission of three to five members is the mediator who has been trying to end the conflict. Often a former mediator is named chairman and the commissioners are always persons thoroughly familiar with the process of collective bargaining. So in this case, with a strike in the metal industry only a few days away, immediate steps are taken to name a commission of arbitration.

Suddenly on December 27 the impasse is ended. Both sides give way sufficiently to make it possible to write a two-year contract containing certain basic wage and hour guarantees in the industry. The general increase was not as large as the union had asked but taken in relation to indices of the cost of living over the past two years it represents nevertheless a real gain and the two weeks' holiday with pay has been conceded. Experts work against time to draw up the formal agreement. It is signed as the old year closes and work continues uninterrupted in the steel industry.

I have simplified this example in order to make clear the way in which the system works. If the last-minute break had not occurred, the conflict would certainly have gone on to a strike. For neither the mediator nor the commission of arbitration has the power to compel a settlement. The mediator may propose that both sides agree to compulsory arbitration and if this proposal is accepted, then the terms fixed by a commission of arbitration become binding.

The basic law creating the office of public mediator was passed in 1906. In the light of experience it has been several times modified, with the role of the mediator given greater importance. In 1920 the law was amended to give the mediator power to call both sides together if the dispute threatened the economic stability of the country. Eleven years later this was strengthened further to make it compulsory upon the mediator to summon both parties, regardless of the seriousness of the dispute.

For the purposes of industrial mediation the country is divided into seven districts with a mediator for each district. These are all part-time jobs which pay about $2,000 a year. Many of the mediators are chosen from the universities but not necessarily among economists or specialists in labor law. For example, the mediator in the fourth district until recently was Hilding Kjellman, a Professor of Romance Languages in the University of Gothenburg. As Gothenburg is the administrative center for the fourth district, Kjellman could devote part of his time to the task of mediation—although occasionally, in the event of a prolonged and difficult dispute, it becomes a full-time job. It is interesting to note that Kjellman was so successful as a mediator that he has left the university for an administrative post, as governor of a northern province.

The only full-time mediator is Olle Ekblom who is also secretary of the division of mediation in the Ministry of Social Affairs. Ekblom follows all important wage negotiations closely, whether in the Stockholm district or elsewhere, and frequently advises the other mediators. He has held his post for more than fifteen years, during which, of course, he has acquired invaluable experience. The public mediators handle each year from 150 to 175 cases, all of which are carefully reported and printed in summary form in a publication of the Ministry of Social Affairs. In 1935 there were 165 disputes that required the intervention of a mediator and for the preceding year the figure was 168. But compared with the number of agreements in force this is not large. The following table shows the collective agreements in effect at the end of 1935 and how they were distributed by industries:

Industries	Number of Agreements	Owners	Number of Workmen
Metallurgy and construction of machines	333	1,151	114,804
Clay and stone industry	303	664	31,626
Lumber industry	813	1,302	92,427
Paper and printing industry . . .	168	633	47,724
Food supply industry	818	2,905	39,679
Textile and clothing industry . .	176	1,081	64,310
Leather, fur, and rubber industry .	225	2,180	22,113
Chemical industry	118	125	9,141
Construction	1,069	5,695	83,129
Public institutions and enterprises .	362	215	47,960
Commerce and warehouses . . .	1,154	1,866	19,626
Transportation on sea and land . .	748	4,003	58,533
Agriculture and fishing	118	1,637	59,896
Other professions	315	3,731	28,465
Total , ...	6,720	27,188	719,433

During this same year 98 wage disputes went to an actual conflict, either a strike or a lockout. The total number of workers involved was 17,189 and the total number of days lost 788,-000. With six exceptions, the conflicts in 1935 were strikes. But 1935 was a good year as a glance at the statistics on wage conflicts for the past three decades quickly shows. In the big strikes that followed the end of the World War, centered around demands for the eight-hour day, nearly nine million working days were lost in 1920 alone. In the big mining strike of 1928 the industry lost 4,835,000 days. More recently, a strike in the building trades that endured from April, 1932, to February, 1933, was largely responsible for the loss of well over six million

working days during the two-year period. The system of re-
newable wage contracts and voluntary mediation is by no means
perfect, as both employers and employees are quick to point out.
That is the reason they have come together in Sweden to discuss
ways and means of improving it. But the process of collective
bargaining follows an orderly and familiar pattern, one which
the public has come to accept. With the possibility that major
wage agreements might be canceled in the fall of 1937, the
Dagens Nyheter, perhaps the leading newspaper in the country,
gave its readers the following sound counsel:

Termination of wage agreements and negotiations for new contracts are normal events in a free labor market, particularly so in
periods of marked prosperity or depression. They signify nothing
especially alarming or disastrous. Therefore it would be foolish, before discussion of the possibility of new agreements has even begun, to make a noise about threatening crises and crashes. Instead
one can calmly hope that reasonable people within all camps will
assist in arriving at an understanding of the actual needs of the
present situation.

One of the major difficulties, and a source of frequent complaint from employers, is in obtaining the assent of the union to
a wage settlement once it has been reached in the course of
negotiations between representatives of both sides. The employers delegate full authority to their negotiators but the unions
have shown great reluctance to take this step. Not infrequently
it happens that an agreement is reached after long and painful
travail, only to be rejected by the votes of a majority of the
members of the union. The whole process must begin again and
this time the union negotiators are at something of a disadvan-
tage. It may happen two or three times, until the other side
finally loses all patience. Union leaders hope that before long it
will be possible to delegate authority to responsible representatives who will then have power to conclude a final agreement
and thus avoid such embarrassments.

What has happened in Denmark during recent years is revealing of the acute crisis that may grow out of a breakdown of
wage negotiations when large numbers of men belonging to a
variety of unions and working for many firms are involved. As

in Sweden, wage negotiations, strikes, and lockouts are conducted according to laws and regulations that have evolved through long experience, going back further, it may be said, in the smaller country.

Because craft boundaries have not been broken down, many unions are customarily involved in negotiation with a single industry in Denmark. Formerly employers could require that each separate union approve the agreement. This sometimes led to serious complications. In 1931 the shoe workers rejected a proposed agreement after the third ballot by a vote so close that the majority in opposition was only 271. The employers took advantage of this situation to declare a lockout against 100,000 workers, members of every union engaged in the negotiation. The federation then announced that it would not support the stand of the shoe workers and the result was that all other union members went back to work and the lockout was maintained only against the group that had persistently voted down an agreement.

The arbitration law was amended in 1934 by the Socialist-Liberal government that has been in power since 1929. Under the amendment the unions involved in a wage negotiation now pool their votes instead of voting separately and the majority of all votes decides the outcome. The majority to reject a proposed wage agreement must be proportionately larger as the number participating in the ballot drops below 75 per cent of the total membership of all unions.

While this solved certain problems, others soon arose. With Denmark's foreign trade in a precarious condition, the effect of any dislocation in industry, particularly in processing and distribution, was certain to be sharply accentuated, reacting upon the whole country. In 1936 the employers in the metal industry rejected the proposal made by Erik Dreyer, chief state mediator. (Under Danish law if a strike or lockout threatens on a large scale, the mediator must propose a settlement unless he concludes that the two sides are so widely separated that it would be useless.) Confronted with what might well have developed into a major crisis, the government then incorporated Dreyer's proposal in a law and recommended it for passage by both chambers of the Parliament.

This was compulsory arbitration and there was an immediate outcry from various quarters. Axel Olsen, head of the largest single union in the country, made up of general factory workers, wrote in the union journal that eventually this would destroy the organized labor movement. It was to be used in this instance against the employers but another time it would be turned on the workers. Social-Democrats, who were also trade-union members, were torn between conflicting loyalties. The party press, the *Social-Demokraten,* reprinted the Olsen article without comment. It was widely rumored that at the party caucus, before a first test vote on the proposed law, the trade-union representatives in Parliament had voted no. But, of course, on the floor they supported the government's measure. However, the government lacked a clear majority in the upper chamber and the proposition was rejected. Instead a law was passed creating a special court of arbitration for this dispute, the decision of this court to be binding upon both sides. The special court created by the emergency law reached a decision that was almost identical with the wage agreement originally put forward by Dreyer, except for the fact that it contained some face-saving devices for the employers. The increase in wages granted by the decision averaged from 4 to 6 per cent.

In 1937 the same situation arose in another important group of industries. Once again the employers rejected the proposal of the state mediator. This time there was no doubt of the government's majority in both chambers and the proposed wage agreement was put in the form of a law and passed in short order. The increase in wages again averaged 4 to 6 per cent.

Quite apart from the wage increases, it is probable that the employers would have rejected the proposed agreement for strategic reasons. For labor has been put in the position of twice resorting to compulsory arbitration. There is no doubt that it is an unhappy precedent. And the Employers' Federation is well aware that it holds a strategic position, particularly should a conservative government come into power again. Within the Employers' Federation some thought was given to the possibility of an attack in the courts on the law compelling arbitration. But it was not considered seriously, for counsel for the federation realized that it could not be argued that the wage increases were confiscatory. In general they were moderate enough and therefore the Supreme Court would never sustain such a challenge. Union leaders are reluctant to discuss the impasse that led to adoption of compulsory arbitration. They say that a similar law applied to the workers would be contrary to basic guarantees since it would, in effect, compel men to labor against their will. For this reason, they are confident, no government would attempt to put through such a law.

There is a growing conviction among critics of the present system that the whole process of arbitration has become too unwieldy, involving too many individuals and organizations, and that therefore it breaks down of its own weight. This point of view is admirably expressed by Jorgen S. Dich, economist of the Ministry of Social Affairs, in a long analysis of the complexities and problems that have arisen in recent years. He concludes that the whole method must be simplified in such a way that local unions and factory groups may be granted a far greater degree of autonomy than they now possess. Localities and even individual factories would negotiate their own wage contracts, avoiding the threat to the entire economic life of the country that arises when wage agreements are terminated through a whole industry on the same date. Permanent compulsory arbitration will come inevitably out of such prolonged and involved disputes, Dich argues. And that will mean the end of the democratic trade-union movement. There is serious concern over this possibility while at the same time those closest to the system of arbitration realize that it will be no easy task to scale it down to a simpler basis.

Recently there have been significant changes although for the most part not in the direction recommended by Dich. The metal industry in Denmark has agreements with some twenty different trade unions. In 1937 for the first time all these unions were represented by a committee of five to whom full authority had been delegated. Politically this was regarded as an important step. In previous years the Employers' Federation dealt with each separate union, taking the skilled workers first. As the unskilled groups were last they usually lost out. Now it is believed it will be possible to obtain a far more equitable wage distribution. In Denmark as in Sweden, trade-union leaders and

Socialists are sharply aware of the need to raise the lowest wage scales.

But once an agreement has been signed, what happens then? What of the innumerable disputes that arise even under the most carefully drawn agreement? In Denmark since 1910 an Industrial Court has existed to settle such disputes, with the power to assess damages against both employers and trade unions. And this court grew out of a voluntary tribunal that was created in 1900 when organized workers and organized employers signed a basic agreement. This first voluntary court, consisting of three representatives of labor and three for industry who then voted upon a chairman, could merely construe the terms of an agreement when disputes arose over its provisions. It lacked the power to assess damages. That came with the law of 1910 which was the result of a decade of experience with a voluntary tribunal.

Trade unions in the Scandinavian countries are not incorporated or registered under law in any way. But there has never been any real question of their responsibility under the law. In general it has been true that if a trade union has drawn up rules, adopted them by majority vote, and conducted its business under these rules, the courts have never denied their legal responsibility.

The present Industrial Court resembles the original one established in 1910. Like that first one, it is made up of three trade-union representatives and three representatives from the Employers' Federation. One representative on each side must be a lawyer and the other four workers and employers respectively. These six elect a chairman each year, a nonpolitical chairman. It is often said of him that he is the only man in Denmark who has no politics. For twelve years the chairman of the court has been V. Topsøe-Jensen who came to his present post from the Supreme Court. The members of the court have no special knowledge of wage agreements. One important function of the Industrial Court is to elect the state mediators.

Obviously it would be impossible for any single court to pass upon all the disputes arising under wage agreements covering several hundred thousand workers. At the same time that the Industrial Court was established in 1910, the basic agreement between the federation of trade unions and the federation of employers was revised to provide for the establishment in each industry of special boards consisting of two representatives from each side and an elected chairman. These boards were set up to pass upon all minor issues and they are particularly well qualified to do so since the members are chosen with a view to their knowledge of the industry.

The Industrial Court itself handles about two hundred cases each year. Under the procedure followed today the chairman hears the case first and in at least one third of the disputes that come before the court he is able to propose a satisfactory settlement without any formal decision from the whole court. The court's chief function, it is stressed by Topsøe-Jensen, is not to condemn or to assess damages but to define the difference between right and wrong.

Thus a wide variety of questions comes before the court. Here, for example, the issue is whether trade unions have given notice of termination of an agreement within the time stipulated in the contract. The court rules that notice has not been given in time and that therefore the agreement must continue in force for another year. Workers in a chocolate factory have been subjected to search and they send their representatives to the court to determine whether or not this is legal. This question the court passes back to the board within the industry because of the need for special knowledge of previous practices and precedents.

The court, that is to say the chairman in virtually every instance, is frequently called upon to pass on the legality of strikes. The law requires two weeks' notice before a strike and once this notice has been given the union comes to the chairman to determine whether the strike will be legal. At times the court may act very quickly. In the event of an illegal strike it may act within a few days. During the term of an agreement there is only one exception to the ban against strikes or lockouts and that is for an action which is in support of other workers on strike or other employers involved in labor trouble. And then only the central organization may call such a sympathy strike or lockout.

One of the reasons why the court has functioned with comparatively little friction, in the opinion of those most familiar with its work, is because the damages assessed have usually been moderate. Both workers and employers complain now and then about a particular decision but they observe the ruling of the court, realizing that it is a general safeguard. It was only during the war and the wave of strikes that occurred during the postwar boom that confidence in the court waned. Otherwise it has held the respect of both sides in the industrial conflict.

Norway, like Denmark, has had an experience with compulsory arbitration. Adopted during the crisis of the World War, it prevailed from 1916 to 1919. Again in 1927 another government, made up of Liberals as was the wartime government, put through a compulsory arbitration law. As in the earlier instance, it was opposed by both employers and employees. In 1928 the state arbitrator announced a settlement in the building trades. The unions refused to accept it and despite the law went out on strike. The same thing happened when a settlement was decreed which the typographical unions rejected. Under the law it was left to the arbitrator to decide when the compulsory clause should be invoked. Confronted with two strikes that enlisted the full support of major unions, it would have been worse than futile to have invoked the compulsory clause. The building strike lasted for seven months and finally on both fronts employers capitulated. No effort was made after that to compel arbitration and the law was formally repealed in 1929.

Norway, more than either Sweden or Denmark, has pushed through legislation which was expected to solve labor problems; legislation which in many instances was hastily conceived and inevitably failed to meet a given situation. The law of 1927 was very broad. It provided not only fines but prison sentences up to three months for a variety of offenses connected with illegal strikes or lockouts.

An Industrial Court more or less on the Danish pattern was established in Norway in 1933 to pass upon disputes under wage agreements. Once a strike or lockout has been declared illegal, the court has merely to fix the amount of damages. Trade unions have not infrequently expelled members who have gone out on an illegal strike, in this way avoiding the payment of damages assessed by the court. Sometimes, as union leaders frankly admit, this is merely a ritual gone through with to get around the law but more often it results when there is an actual disagreement between the leadership and the rank and file. It follows that if leaders of the union come into court and say first that they have been unable to prevent the strike and finally that they have expelled the members, then no damages can be assessed.

The law was put to an interesting test in 1936. Prices were rising rapidly and in July there were sixteen illegal strikes, most of them in the building trades. Union representatives went to the employers to say that they could expel their members who were out on strike contrary to the terms of wage agreements still in force but they added that the movement was so strong among the rank and file that this action would leave almost no one to carry on building operations. Realizing that this was an impossible situation, the employers gave in, granted the demands of the strikers and no damages were assessed by the court. The court acts only on complaint of one side or the other.

In the same year that the Industrial Court was established, a boycott law was passed. The Farmers' party, later to conclude a working alliance with the Socialists but at the time openly hostile to labor, was in power. Outlawing seven specific types of boycott, it made it virtually impossible to use this weapon. And the boycott had been extremely useful to the trade-union movement. The law was particularly aimed at the "conditioned boycott," that is, a threat to boycott Firm A unless it ceases to do business with Firm B against which a strike is being conducted. A special boycott court to hear complaints was established at the same time but the law itself is so formidable that this court has had almost nothing to do. Considerable discussion over repeal of this law has brought little result. The labor representation in the upper chamber of Parliament is now only 71 and a majority is 76. To get enough extra votes for repeal it would be necessary to make important concessions and it is doubtful that this will be done.

The traditions of a free labor movement are so strong in Sweden that the idea of an Industrial Court with the power to declare strikes illegal and assess damages against a union was long resisted. It was pointed out that there had already been created a fairly extensive voluntary machinery, within the terms of most wage contracts, to take care of disputes arising when an agreement was in force. These wage contracts carried clauses providing for the arbitration of differences arising during the course of the year or two years that they were effective. Some contracts still provide definite rules whereby disputes are to be referred to a central organization for settlement.

Nevertheless there was persistent agitation for a labor court, a good deal of it arising from sources suspicious of organized labor. When such a court was proposed by a Liberal government in 1928, there was fierce opposition from labor even though by the terms of the proposed law the jurisdiction of the court was to be strictly limited to disputes arising under a contract, with no authority whatsoever over the conduct of wage negotiations or the arbitration of wage differences between contracts.

The Social-Democrats put on a great demonstration in the streets of Stockholm, thousands of marchers, flags flying, and the leader of the party, Per Albin Hansson, at the head of the procession. The opposition was of no avail, the law was passed and the court established to function along the lines of the Danish Industrial Court. Today trade-union leaders will concede privately that in general the decisions of the court have not harmed organized labor or hampered the growth of the movement as had been direly prophesied in 1928. Publicly there are still occasional protests but they seem to lack real conviction.

Here is the Industrial Court in action. It is a big, formal room in the Rådhus, the Law Courts building at Stockholm. At the head of the broad table under the low-hanging crystal chandelier sits Arthur Lindhagen, chairman of the court, a former judge of the Supreme Court. On opposite sides are the other members of the court, two neutral members named by the Crown, as is the chairman, two representatives for labor, and two for the employers.

This case is particularly interesting, for it has to do with a conflict between the City of Stockholm, as employer, and certain municipal employees, members of the union of communal workers. The fixed working place agreed to in the wage contract with this group of workers is Mälar wharf and those who have been called upon to do occasional work, such as the maintenance of ports and bridges at some distance from the wharf, are given for a total of six days following their transfer to a new job a special allowance of 40 cents a day. The union is demanding that the six-day limit be abolished. First the union representative is called to the witness chair to tell that side of the story. "Those who are called outside the working radius, with the wharf as a center, must pay for their lunches and their streetcar fares," he says. "But if you were transferred to another job for some period of time, say six months, you wouldn't expect this extra compensation, would you?" Chairman Lindhagen asks. The answer is yes. A representative of the city replies that this extra compensation was not intended to be permanent but under the contract it was to be superseded on a day's notice of transfer to a more distant job.

The hearing in this case requires less than an hour and the court has time at the morning session to hear a second case, a conflict between the Seamen's Union and the Swedish Shippers' Association. There are lawyers to present both sides in this dispute which has to do with overtime work performed by sailors while in port. The union is claiming an extra half-hour's pay for every day in port to cover certain duties that were unforeseen at the time the contract was drawn up.

The court adjourns at 12.30 for the day. It meets only twice a month and yet in normal times there are so few disputes requiring formal adjudication that the court is not hard pressed. And decisions are rendered promptly, within a week or ten days after the case has been taken under advisement.

The system of fixed wage contracts, negotiated through collective bargaining, is, as I have said, far from perfect. For one thing it is extraordinarily complex, requiring what sometimes seems a fantastic degree of supervision and coöperation. The wage agreement in the transport industry in Norway illustrates this complexity. At least six weeks are required for the negotiation which includes a separate wage scale for workers in the shipping industry at every port along Norway's deeply indented coast. Once this process has been gone through, the varying wage scales are printed in a thick book.

This is the way many Swedish workers spend a great deal of their leisure time, working on a boat instead of an automobile.

The same thing is true in the building industry. Here the variance between hourly rates and piecework is a complicating factor. A booklet of 144 pages printed in fine type contains the rates for building carpenters in Sweden for the year 1937. There is no need to dwell upon the opportunities for disagreement that such a system affords. To pass upon piecework rates in Stockholm and other large cities two representatives, one from the Employers' Federation and one from the union, go from one building job to another. In the event of a dispute each must report back his findings. It sometimes seems like a very elaborate kind of game with a set of rules so lengthy and complicated that no one umpire could ever comprehend them.

As to the final effect of the system, one hears far fewer complaints from businessmen than from trade unionists. Over a fairly long period of years it is possible to show a definite and very marked increase in real wages. But trade-union leaders find that it is more and more difficult to achieve any appreciable gain. They fear that the wage level has become stabilized. This has become increasingly true as the cost of living index has become a more and more important factor in wage negotiations.

In April and May, 1937, major wage agreements in Norway were revised. Most of the new contracts called for an increase of 10 per cent. This covered the rise in the cost of living that had occurred during the two years the previous agreements were in force. And therefore, as union leaders pointed out, it was no real gain. The new contracts were also for two years, to run until April and May of 1939. They all contain, however, a provision that if the cost of living index reaches a certain figure, then the trade unions may demand a revision of the contract. With prices rising rapidly through the summer of 1937, it was thought it would perhaps be necessary to invoke the cost of living clause before the agreements had run a year. But the down trend that set in toward the close of the year postponed this for a time at least.

Those who are somewhat detached from the actual conflict are more optimistic about future gains. The Norwegian public mediator, who has had many years' experience with collective bargaining, holds that the wage level is far from stabilized. The past two decades, he insists, have seen marked gains, with a rise of 40 to 50 per cent in the real standard of living since 1914.

It is true that the trade unions have had no concerted wage policy. There has been little or no recognition of the relation of wages to other elements in the economy. For the most part each group has simply gone out to get the biggest possible share of the total sum that industry pays out each year in wages. The result has been that unskilled workers and those who were poorly organized have received a disproportionately small share of total wages.

Now the Swedish trade-union movement, the most advanced of the three, has begun to try to shape an entirely new wage policy; one which will take into account the whole varying scale of wages from the lowest paid unskilled workers to the craft aristocrats. In the past the financial resources of the federation have been available under certain rather narrow restrictions to aid individual unions in prosecuting strikes. It is the intention under the new wage policy to use the funds of the federation where they will be most effective in supporting the drive to raise the pay of workers at the bottom of the scale. This was made clear in Lindberg's first speech to the federation in which he warned that individual unions might have to sacrifice something of the autonomy they had hitherto enjoyed.

Among the leaders at least there is a strong awareness that it is no longer possible to ignore other groups and other classes in the community. Friendly advances have been made to the separate federation DACO (*De anställdas centralorganisation*), which is made up of trade unions of white-collar workers. While certain jurisdictional questions remain unsettled between the trade-union federation and DACO, there is no hostility between them, and future policy looks toward the achievement of a gradual rapprochement of some sort. In the same way trade-union leaders have thrown their support behind the movement, both through government and through labor organization, for higher wages for farm and forest workers.

Certainly there is middle-class antagonism toward the trade unions. Part of this grows out of the vigor with which strikes are prosecuted by the trade unions. A strike means a "blockade" against the offending employer, an attempt to shut off any possible source of obtaining workers. It means not only a boycott of the firm itself but a secondary boycott aimed at those firms and individuals that continue to do business with the offender. There is careful organization behind the strike and detailed direction and supervision once it has been declared.

But with one exception, and that has been generally ascribed to a tragic blunder, there is no violence in Sweden's labor history. Racketeering in trade unions in the American sense is unheard of and so is the labor spy employed by industry. Such practices seem to the Scandinavians incomprehensible. Even when the conflict was at its height, in the first decade of this century, rules and regulations were observed.

A great deal of the middle-class antagonism that exists is directed at the building unions. Struggling bank clerks and small professional people sincerely believe the stories that are the current coin of anti-union propaganda in every country . . . a man is not allowed to paint his own house or repair his own roof. It is true that the most serious conflicts of recent years have arisen in the building industry. And the nearest thing to a sit-down strike occurred in this same industry. This manifestation of labor's insurgence shocked a great many Swedes.

Although wage agreements were in force in 1934 and 1935 building workers frequently called sporadic strikes without any authorization from union headquarters, "quickies," to use the American term. Often these isolated strikes would grow out of a dispute on a particular job over piece rates. There would be an impasse in the argument and the workers would sit down in the booths provided for their shelter and general well-being on every large building job. "Sit-in-the-booth" was the Swedish phrase applied to this practice.

Employers complain that even when the Industrial Court has handed down a decision outlawing a strike it is difficult to enforce the letter of the law. Bricklayers employed by the Swedish tobacco monopoly went on strike and declared a blockade. The issue was whether they should be searched as they left the factory. The court ruled the strike was illegal and ordered the blockade ended. Officially the union complied. But a representative of the Federation of Building Trades' Employers complained that in private the word still circulated and it was difficult to obtain sufficient workers to finish the construction job. Undoubtedly the complexity that characterizes wage rates and wage agreements has something to do with the public attitude.

From the point of view of public interest and convenience the most serious labor dispute in the last two years was that involving employers and employees in hotels and restaurants in principal cities. Hotel and restaurant personnel demanded substantial wage increases and abolition of tipping. For certain categories of work the increases ranged from 20 to 40 per cent and were generally felt to be unreasonable. For weeks negotiations continued and still the two sides were a long way apart. The intervention first of state arbitrators and then later of a commission of arbitration was fruitless. Trade-union negotiators would not yield on major points and finally the Employers' Association decided to declare a lockout.

Even smaller restaurants not directly involved in the dispute joined in the sympathy lockout and in Stockholm alone more than four hundred cafés closed their doors. The big hotels turned out their guests, the last to go surrendering their keys with a ceremonial finality that was duly recorded in the press. The last night before cafés and night clubs were to close was like New Year's Eve, with huge crowds and much gaiety.

There were virtually no exceptions to the united front presented by hotel and restaurant employers. The café in the House of Parliament was closed, as were the Norma temperance restaurants which are operated on a nonprofit basis. For travelers and visitors compelled to remain in the city over a considerable period the situation presented a serious problem. It was with remarkable good nature that the public at large accepted the dilemma.

Members of Parliament in the capital for the current session were particularly inconvenienced. And yet they, too, preserved, as the account in the *Dagens Nyheter* put it, an Olympian calm. Governor Johan Nilsson, chairman of the first chamber, insisted that he would continue to live at the Grand Hotel as he always had, lockout or no lockout. It would be possible, he explained, to bring in food from nearby delicatessens. And as for heat, if the heating plant was shut down he would simply buy a sleeping bag and camp out. It would be more comfortable after all than camping out in the far north which he had done many times. Cartoonists and caricaturists had a field day. They depicted members of Parliament looking enviously at one or two of their colleagues who had had the foresight to bring their lunches.

The lockout will cause inconvenience [the liberal *Dagens Nyheter* said, taking the "common sense" line], but it is unreasonable to talk about this as a socially dangerous conflict. Take the thing calmly. From the general point of view it is fortunate above all that the fight did not take place during the tourist season. The employers have started a general lockout at this time, it is obvious, in order to force an agreement before the spring and summer season.

Above all no attempt will be made to enforce arbitration. The hotel and restaurant personnel apparently had a chance to obtain peaceably a higher wage scale, gains actually greater than those won by workers in other lines at the turn of the year. This being the case, it is doubly to be deplored that a conflict costly and troublesome for all sides could not have been avoided.

For the union the conflict was extremely serious. The cost to the union, according to the treasurer, was not less than 200,000 kronor a week, most of which went to pay benefits to members who were locked out. Nevertheless the union line held for more than six weeks. Begun toward the end of January, the lockout was not called off until negotiations were finally concluded on March 12. The contract agreed upon provided an average wage increase of about 12 per cent, with specific raises for every category except those most highly paid. Included in the general terms were provisions for improved vacation and health compensation. While the tipping question was not solved, the contract called for higher guaranteed wages for waiters and further discussion of the issue.

Once again as cafés and night clubs reopened the Stockholmers celebrated. There were large crowds everywhere and a gala atmosphere as diners-out sought out favorite tables in favorite restaurants after the long interval of enforced absence. The lockout had not served to endear the Restaurant Employers' Association with a public given to dining out. A strong feeling prevailed that it was unfair to insist upon the closing of restaurants that were not unionized and also chains like Norma operated at cost in lower middle-class sections of the city.

There was, it appears, an underlying political motive. In part the lockout was a protest against the law adopted the previous year by the labor government taking away all profit on the sale of liquor in restaurants. This was to be done gradually over a period of twenty-five years but nevertheless it caused widespread resentment, and the employers apparently decided to show their independence.

One reason the negotiations broke down, in the view of neutral observers, was that both sides to the dispute were comparatively new to the technique of collective bargaining. Older and more experienced negotiators might have avoided the impasse. The *Social-Demokraten* took a curious line, championing the rights of the mythical "third party" . . . the public at large. The lockout was violating these rights, it was argued, and the "third party" was the real victim of the strike. This has been the protest of the Right in the face of large-scale strikes. And the response of the conservatives to the editorials in the *Social-Demokraten,* a response which might have been foreseen, was not long in coming. Conservative leaders immediately demanded that legal limitations be put upon labor conflicts. If the "third party" suffered in a lockout, then surely, it was argued, a strike must also cause suffering and therefore the time was ripe to curb all such excesses.

While the motives behind this reasoning were plain enough, it is true that on the Left as well as on the Right there is a widespread realization of the need to improve and extend the methods of collective bargaining. In a highly sensitive economy, with an ever-increasing degree of state intervention, a strike or a lockout appears as an impossible reversion to the primitive. Various tentative ways are being experimented with to avoid such crises. A new way of bargaining was tried out in 1938, bargaining in advance of the date when notice of cancellation of the wage contract must be given. The advantages are obvious. What is more the unions in the printing industry signed a wage contract for eight years during which no strike or lockout will be possible. The contract provides that at the end of each two-year period the wage scale shall be submitted to an arbitration commission, the findings of the commission to be binding on both sides.

These are tentative steps in the direction of a more lasting form of labor peace. All the more familiar processes of collective bargaining the public in general has long since come to accept as a part of everyday life. Within limits the business of bargaining for wages has brought marked gains for the workers. It has been on the political front, however, that labor has bargained for a larger share of the national income, insisting that the state must make up for the deficiencies in distribution that result in monopoly and the concentration of wealth.

CHAPTER IV

THE LABOR GOVERNMENTS

IN Sweden, Norway, and Denmark labor governments are in power. The difficulties of the task they face from day to day could scarcely be exaggerated. Subject to varied and conflicting pressures both from within the country and without, they must reconcile these forces and steer a careful parliamentary course. When to yield, when to stand firm, how much to surrender, what is worth a last ditch fight, these are questions that daily perplex labor ministers of the Scandinavian states. In a world increasingly given over to absolutism they seek to govern by reason, the democratic method, realizing all the time that a political democracy cannot continue to exist unless it is possible to achieve a larger measure of economic democracy.

And to make the task even more complicated, they are not in power as the result of an outright labor majority. It was only thanks to the supporting votes of Farmers and Liberals that they were able to form their governments. In Sweden there has finally grown out of this collaboration an outright Farmer-Labor coalition. But in Norway and Denmark the Social-Democrats stay in power at the sufferance of other parties. This support is uncertain; it may be withdrawn over any issue. Such uncertainty is not conducive to the formulation of a long-range program. Nevertheless in the face of recurring world crises and economic breakdown these governments have been remarkably successful. Thus far they have ridden out the storm. One must add, however, that there are numerous critics who insist that they have yielded far too much in order to survive.

In Denmark this survival seems little short of miraculous. Since 1929 the Social-Democratic government of Prime Minister Stauning has been in power, supported by the votes of the Radical-Lefts, a party bearing some resemblance to the Radical-Socialist party of France, if only in the fact that it is neither radical nor very far to the Left. During the period that the Stauning government has been in power the Danes have been confronted with a major shift in world trade, which has meant drastic adjustments at home. And yet in two elections, in 1932 and in 1935, the Social-Democrats have increased their majority. Out of twelve members of the cabinet today, only three are Radical Lefts, the others Laborites.

Actually Denmark today is in a most unhappy position. The long shadow of Nazi Germany lies dark over the land. To survive at all it has been necessary, in the interpretation of the government in power, to accept what amounts almost to German hegemony. Outwardly there has been no change, or at least no change that the foreign visitor is made immediately aware of. But in the other Scandinavian countries they are acutely conscious of the plight of the Danes.

Critics of the present regime in Denmark see many unfortunate parallels between the Social-Democratic party that governs the country today and the Social-Democratic party that flourished in neighboring Germany prior to the advent of Hitler. Like its German counterpart, it has been built upon a trade-union bureaucracy. Over a period of thirty years, during which the party has gradually widened the sphere of its influence from municipal to central government, a legion of bureaucrats and public officeholders has come into being. At a time of crisis when radical adjustments are plainly necessary, they tend to think in terms of survival, clinging to the perquisites and privileges of the officeholder, of those who have a vested interest in the *status quo*.

Deeply rooted in the past, the organization of the Social-Democratic party is thorough and painstaking. Take the newspapers that it operates throughout the country. There are sixty-four separate editions of the *Social-Demokraten*. In a sense these are separate newspapers, each with its own editor, varying in importance from that published in the capital to the *Social-Demokraten* of the smallest village. But they are built around seventeen central organizations in which all sixty-four papers are printed. In each of these central offices is an editor-in-chief who has immediate supervision over the papers in his area. The same syndicated articles and features are used in many instances in all the papers. The result of this remarkable organization is a total circulation of nearly 200,000, considerably more than that of any other newspaper in the country.

Yet one finds a growing dissatisfaction with these party dailies. The younger generation complains that they are written and edited in accord with an outmoded pattern, a narrow party line. They reflect, one is told, a dull sectarianism that is characteristic of the bureaucrats who control the party itself. What is plain is that traditionalism weighs heavily upon the party press. Little understanding of the desires and demands of the average newspaper reader goes into the editing of these *Social-Demokraten*. Party funds are doled out grudgingly to support the press. The result is that the *Social-Demokraten* of Copenhagen compares unfavorably with such an excellent and aggressive newspaper as the liberal *Politiken*.

Party leaders are aware of a mounting dissatisfaction. There has been a serious attempt to modernize party practices and above all to enlarge the scope of the party. A special organization exists to attract youth. As will be seen in a later chapter, there has been an effort to draw the middle class into trade unions and support of labor organization and labor government. Even if it were not for the mounting criticism that has been expressed both within and without the country, the mistakes of the German Social-Democracy are too recent to be ignored; that deadly sectarianism, the stubborn identification of the "proletariat" with a class that was in reality a privileged class, preoccupation with empty doctrine and empty form. Social-Democrats in Denmark are aware of what these symptoms mean and they are trying to make over their party. But it is difficult to throw off the habits, and particularly the habits of thought, of fifty years.

This is demonstrated clearly in the way in which the government has met the crises of the past ten years. What has happened to Denmark, where life was so intelligently and precisely ordered, seems cruel indeed. Blame for the fact that Germany has established a kind of protectorate over her small neighbor must be placed in considerable degree on Great Britain. It goes back to the narrow and stupid policy of empire self-sufficiency typified by the phrase, "Buy British!"

In Denmark the principal industry is farming. It has been developed to such a point of efficiency and standardization that even an American motor manufacturer might learn something from a Danish farm coöperative. With virtually the highest per capita rate of export in Europe, three fourths of the products that the Danes send into world trade are from the farms. This farm export has been essential to maintain the high standard of living that has prevailed in both rural and urban areas.

When the Laborites came into power in Denmark in 1929, on a platform of mild reformism, they were confronted almost at once with a sharp disparity between the price of farm products and the price of manufactured products. And ever since, the Danes have had to sell their bacon and eggs and butter in a cheap world market and buy manufactured consumers' goods in a dear market. The result has been a scramble, oftentimes a desperate scramble, for foreign exchange and foreign credits.

As though this situation was not difficult enough in itself, the Beaverbrooks of Great Britain have succeeded through their "Buy British" campaign in cutting Danish exports to nearly half of what they had been in normal, predepression years. Hard pressed for foreign credits in the face of this loss, the Social-Democratic government has lived in fear and trembling of further losses. The export trade to Germany has taken on as a result an overwhelming significance. The mere hint of a threat to curtail or abolish this trade has in numerous instances been sufficient to bring the government to terms. In 1936 one fourth of all Danish imports came from Germany and of total exports one fifth went to the neighbor on the south. In the same year Great Britain took slightly more than half of all Danish exports and Denmark received from the British Isles somewhat more than a third of all her imports. These proportions were not substantially altered in 1937.

The foreign trade dilemma has had the most far-reaching effect on internal policy. In 1934 there was a strike in the slaughter houses. When it had gone on for a week, a telegram came from British trade interests demanding to know whether or not the strike would interfere with shipments of Danish bacon. There was an implied threat that Britain would turn elsewhere for food imports should the strike effect the flow of trade between the two countries. The government thereupon rushed through a measure outlawing the strike. The trade with Great Britain was an absolute necessity and nothing could be allowed to interfere with it. That was the compulsion behind the passage of the law.

The pressure from Germany is almost constant, under the threat that trade with Denmark will be curtailed. If a particularly sharp attack on Hitler or the Nazis appears in *Politiken,* which is banned from Germany, the Foreign Office is very likely to hear of it. Not directly, perhaps, but German interests will make representations to Danish interests and the protest is forwarded to Dr. Munch, the Foreign Minister. Poor Dr. Munch, a Radical-Left, is made very unhappy by these protests.

What he does on these occasions is to call the important journalists together in his office for tea. They gather politely and solemnly, knowing very well what the reason for the meeting is. The conversation is general until at last Dr. Munch raises the question which all in the room have known was the reason for their presence. The article in *Politiken,* says the Foreign Minister, has caused a great deal of unpleasantness. The Wilhelmstrasse is distinctly annoyed and has expressed its annoyance through the firm of X which has in turn passed the word on to the Danish firm of Y. Everyone knows, the good doctor goes on, how vital is the trade with Germany, how dependent the whole national economy is upon this trade. Of course, there is nothing like a censorship in Denmark but isn't it possible to avoid writing that kind of an article? Particularly when the situation is so delicate? Dr. Munch looks round at the assembled journalists appealingly. There is a faintly murmured response which seems to mean neither an affirmative nor a negative and the conversation, to the great relief of everyone, passes back to polite generalities.

These little sessions in Dr. Munch's spacious rose-and-gilt office are a kind of symbol of the foreboding fears that obsess the Danes today. And it is not as though they were rare and infrequent; these meetings have occurred during recent years as often as once a month. Another unhappy sign is the praise for the Danish military establishment that appears in German army and navy journals. The indication clearly is that Denmark has come to terms with her powerful neighbor. In a speech at Lund in Sweden in the fall of 1937, Prime Minister Stauning emphatically rejected any sort of military alliance with the other Scandinavian countries for the preservation of neutrality.

It must be remembered that the Danes live on the very doorstep of Nazi Germany. Any increase in armaments looking to an alliance with Sweden, Norway, and Finland would have been immediately interpreted by the Germans as a hostile act. Trade reprisals would in all probability have followed. Perhaps it was inevitable from the first that this small country should come under the influence of a Germany bent on remaking Europe. Prime Minister Stauning thunders against the threat of Communist Russia almost as though he were himself a member in good standing of Hitler's government.

There are clever young people on the Left, not Communists so much as Left-Socialists, who insist that another line might just possibly have saved the country from such a complete capitulation to Nazi power. They criticize the Stauning government for having accepted the *status quo* in trade relationships. The government might have extended credits to private firms to encourage the expansion of domestic industry and in so doing might have made the national economy somewhat less dependent on imports from Britain and Germany. There was no effort to make any fundamental readjustment of the economy. Once the fact of dependence upon German trade was accepted as inevitable, all the consequences of what is practically German hegemony followed.

Perhaps because they themselves are so acutely aware of the unfortunate situation which confronts them today, the Danes are hypersensitive to criticism. Johan Vogt, a Norwegian Left-Wing journalist, wrote for Oslo's Socialist *Arbeiderbladet* a series of very searching articles on the plight of Denmark. While these articles were critical, they were not unfriendly. And yet they produced a storm of indignation in Denmark. The attitude of the Danish Social-Democrats was that Vogt had committed an act of disloyalty. An analytical article in a French newspaper actually drew a protest from the Foreign Office.

A complicating factor in Denmark is the farm situation. There has never been any working alliance between city Laborites and farmers. In fact, as will be shown in a later chapter, there has been an underlying hostility between these two basic groups. The volume of farm exports dwindled and, as has been noted, at the same time there was an increasing disproportion between the price of those farm staples Denmark sends into the world and the manufactured products she must buy. The scarcity of foreign credits has made it necessary to put sharp restrictions on purchases abroad. There is a more or less rigid quota on motor cars, not only as to the number that can be imported but on the price range as well. And the same thing applies in other fields of manufacture. On the preferred list of imports absolute necessities come first, such necessities as fertilizer and chemicals. Denmark, it must be remembered, is a country almost entirely without mineral resources.

Not only geographically but intellectually and emotionally the Danes are much more intimately a part of Europe than their first cousins in Norway and Sweden. Even the casual traveler is made aware of this in going from the Scandinavian peninsula to the little country that lies across the narrow gray sound. Copenhagen is a far more sophisticated city than Stockholm. There is about it a quality of gaiety, almost nervous gaiety one is inclined to say, that is lacking in the placid capital of the Swedes.

This is reflected in a measure in the government. The Danish Social-Democrats are far more given to airs and graces than their Swedish counterparts. Prime Minister Stauning is noted for his gray top hats and the splendor of his waistcoats. He lives more nearly in the manner of the *haute bourgeoisie* than Per Albin Hansson who each night takes the street car to his little home in suburban Äppelviken, outside Stockholm. Stauning is fond of being seen at the opera and at Copenhagen's brilliant restaurants.

These outward manifestations may seem trivial but they are not without significance. Socialist ministers, they live in a world of opulent blandishments. This is what happens. Minister Blank and his wife are invited to the beautiful country place of the Count and Countess X. There are a half dozen guests, charming people. The appointments are perfect, the week-end a great success. "Don't you think," says one of the Danish guests to the American visitor, "that Countess X was clever to invite Minister

Blank?" Hospitable and kindly, yes, but clever? "Clever, of course, for he has seen how attractive and graceful our life is and when it comes to a new tax bill to destroy us, he will find it more difficult to approve."

Having failed to win by ballots, the upper class seeks to convert the victors. The example of Great Britain and the labor ministers who succumbed to snobbism is still very recent. There are so many rewards that the owning class can hold out and they have, in European civilization at least, the weight of age and tradition on their side.

A story, whether apocryphal or not is of no importance since it fits his character, is told about one of the first labor ministers in Sweden, in the cabinet of Hjalmar Branting. At a large official reception he was approached by a very patronizing aristocrat whose chief pride is the fact that his title antedates that of King Gustaf by several centuries. "I understand," he said after a few minutes of conversation, "that you began life as a cobbler. How very extraordinary." "Yes, that's correct," said the minister, "a very good trade. But I'm afraid you wouldn't care for it. And therefore it's good you didn't begin life as a cobbler. Because if you had, you would still be a cobbler." This was said in an amiable, matter-of-fact way.

While the Social-Democratic parties of Denmark and Sweden are nominally socialist, they have become in reality parties of reform. One hears little of socialization even at election time. The Social-Democrats have fostered all the reforms—old-age pensions, workmen's compensation insurance, mass housing, state medicine, unemployment relief and public works—that mark the efforts of democracy to adjust to the modern world. The Social-Democrats have had this field almost entirely to themselves and in the interpretation of Ernst Wigforss, Minister of Finance, it is the real reason for Sweden's success. The conservatives in Sweden and Denmark have not yet learned the strategy that the Tories of Great Britain have been practicing for many years; that is, to pass out social benefits (in moderation) while the parties on the Left are talking about them.

During four years of steadily increasing prosperity, from 1933 to 1936, the Social-Democrats were in power in Sweden. In the elections that were held in the fall of the latter year they came

for the first time within a few votes of an outright majority,
polling well over half of the total vote cast. The methods used
in that election are revealing of the nature of the party.

During the entire campaign, for at least two months prior to
election day, there was a constant flow of propaganda that was
simple, direct, and yet appealing and shrewd. Huge posters,
pamphlets, special newspapers, motion picture films, all stressed
the same claim: the Workers' party is for a job for everyone,
security, better homes, better schools, larger old-age pensions, a
higher standard of living. In a thousand concrete ways this
theme was illustrated. A smiling woman with a child on her
arm looks out from the doorway of a state-subsidized home.
"Healthy Homes for Poor Children," is the legend, "Vote with
the Workers' Party." Another poster says: "Three Just Demands—Healthy Homes for Children—Larger Pensions for the
Aged—A Job and Security for All."

As political parties all over the world have done since the beginning of time, the Social-Democrats capitalized on the rise in
prosperity that had occurred during their term in office. A striking poster dramatized the statistics of unemployment in Sweden, England, Holland, and France for the four years from
1933 to 1936. The sharp decrease in Sweden stood out in striking contrast to what had happened in the other three countries.
Both Holland and France showed a marked rise in unemployment during the period. The legend beneath was: "The decline
of unemployment in Sweden is without parallel. Our land finds
itself in a class by itself. Why? It is the result of a sensible
policy pursued in the crisis."

One of the most striking posters informed the voters that the
Workers' party obtained a 50 per cent increase in old-age pensions in 1935. And it was only the "bourgeois parties," the legend went on, that prevented another increase in 1936. This and
other pension posters were illustrated with the photographs of a
nice old man and woman, their beaming smiles called forth apparently by a larger pension. A whole series of posters set forth
the public works carried out by the Social-Democrats; so many
thousand homes modernized with state funds, so many thousand dwellings built with state subsidies, so many bridges constructed, so many hundred kilometers on the state railway elec-

trified, so many grade crossings eliminated, harbors improved, and so on. As a matter of fact it would be an impressive list for a much larger and more populous country.

The election propaganda of the Social-Democrats is not, of course, all of this elemental type. Considerable emphasis is placed upon the concentration of ownership in a comparatively few hands. One of the pamphlets widely circulated during the campaign was *The Dominion of High Finance* by Frans Severin, one of the foremost economists and thinkers in the party. In this pamphlet Severin pointed to the numerous interlocking directorates through which certain bankers, and conspicuously the Wallenberg family, controlled a large portion of Swedish industry. One Social-Democratic poster ridiculed the factional quarrels between the Left Socialists, containing the remnants of the Syndicalist party, under the leadership of Kilbom, and the Communists. Two figures on an election platform are shown alternately embracing and assaulting each other.

Separate leaflets were prepared for each province showing over a period of years how the proportion of Social-Democratic voters had increased and urging party workers to make the percentage even larger at the coming election. The pamphlets for every province contained a paragraph on the general situation. "The total number of votes this year will be about 3,900,000. Of this number 2,200,000 belong to the working class and therefore there is a good chance for a sharp increase in the total of Social-Democratic votes."

When the final vote was counted, it was seen that the hopes of even the most enthusiastic Laborites had been outstripped. The leaders of the party decided against attempting, however, to form an independent government with the tacit support of small Leftist fractions in the Parliament. Instead they agreed to continue their collaboration with the farmers, both Farm party and Labor party to accept joint responsibility for policies laid down.

That is the government which now rules Sweden. At times, one suspects, the Social-Democrats would welcome a somewhat more vigorous opposition. On the Left the Syndicalist party is melting away and Kilbom has just been admitted to the ranks of the Social-Democrats. The party of the Right spends most of its time viewing with shocked alarm which decidedly mitigates its usefulness. Perhaps the most effective line of opposition is that taken by the liberal People's party.

Although this party has polled at recent elections only a small percentage of the vote, it has been reanimated by its leaders. Men such as Gustaf H. Anderson, Rasjön, and Professor Bertil Ohlin have denounced the Social-Democrats for not going far enough with their reforms. At a big rally in the north of Sweden in the summer of 1937 Ohlin berated the government for its timidity, advocating at the same time a series of drastic changes in education, public works, and a number of . other fields. Here, of course, he came up against the Swedish temperament which is unreceptive to sudden and startling innovations.

The same tactic tried in Parliament has occasionally caused embarrassment. In the finance committee of the second chamber a Liberal member denounced the allocation of the government for a particular social service. After this had gone on for some time, the Social-Democrats on the committee hit upon a shrewd bit of strategy. All right, they said, it may be true that this is too slow and therefore let us follow the advice of our friend, let's double it. This proposal, made in all seriousness, was sufficient to call the Liberal member's bluff and he subsided into silence.

Nevertheless the strategy of the Liberals shows an insight into the dilemma of the party in power. It is a question of how fast and how far to go. There are those within the Social-Democratic party, among them some of the keenest and most intelligent young leaders, who feel that the present period of comparative prosperity and peace is passing with too little accomplished. They hold that far more drastic measures are necessary if the party is to retain its mass following in the next crisis. Those who are responsible for policy are reluctant to disturb the present tranquillity. Business in the spring of 1938 was still at a high level and unemployment at a minimum. The budget was overbalanced and the national debt rapidly contracting. In view of all this the government abated its demands for social and economic reforms. Unofficially there was declared a breathing spell. But in the view of younger and more ardent party members it was precisely the time for action rather than delay.

There were, of course, some social laws. One was the measure granting a twelve-day holiday with full pay to all manual and clerical workers in the country. Within the last two years collective agreements have stipulated annual holidays of less than six working days for 60 per cent of all workers; only 26 per cent had six days and only 6 per cent twelve days. In certain respects therefore the new law is a radical one. The customary vacation of white-collar workers is two weeks, lengthened to three after a certain term of service and finally to a month. Civil servants have a month's holiday, and through an agreement made between the newspapers and the union of journalists all newspaper editorial workers have a similar vacation with pay after they have been employed a year.

What critics of the present cautious policy have in mind is an attack on certain fundamental problems, particularly those centering around housing. Ground rents and building costs are still so high that overcrowding is inevitable. There are state subsidies to coöperative building societies, particularly for families with many children. The city of Stockholm has its own ingenious plan of small house construction.* But there has been no far-reaching effort to get at the basic causes of the housing dilemma.

It is curious how all over the world one comes up against this business of housing. Partly it is traceable to the World War. In Stockholm, as in almost every other large city in Europe and America, there was an acute wartime shortage of dwellings and property values soared. They have never come down to anything like the prewar level. A tax structure is based in part upon inflated land values, services and institutions are built upon these values and change becomes increasingly difficult.

Another factor is the high hourly wage rate that prevails in the building industry, in Sweden as in the United States and Great Britain. Yet the annual wage of building workers is often very low. A study of employment in the building industry made by the Carpenters' Union showed that no building car-

* For fuller discussion see *Sweden: The Middle Way.*

penters worked the total number of hours possible in a year—
2,400—and only a comparatively few worked 2,300 hours in
the year. Some averaged as few as 600 and even 400 hours.

But leaders of the building unions insist that an annual wage
is for practical reasons impossible. To begin with there can be
no control over the weather. Nor will it be possible to control
the volume of building from year to year, the pessimists say.
Conservative trade unionists in the building industry are against
anything that seems to threaten even a small part of their province. They oppose the Stockholm plan of small house construction, which calls for a certain number of hours of labor on the
part of the family acquiring the dwelling. Building workers con-
tend that this spare time labor on the part of householders de-
prives them of work and tends to jeopardize the union wage
scale. It is from the coöperative building society, known as
H.S.B. (from the Swedish Hyresgästernas Sparkassa och Byg-
gnads-förening), that the principal drive for an annual wage in
the industry has come. A national committee has been named
by the government to report on the problem of rationalization
of the whole building industry and action will wait upon the report of that committee.

Members of the government, and particularly the Prime Minister, Per Albin Hansson, are sensitive to criticism that their
policy has been too cautious. When Norman Thomas and other
American Socialists come to see Per Albin, they invariably ask
him when the government is to begin the socialization of the
nation's industries. And what he tells them, not without a certain impatience, is that the government is building socialism
into the fabric of the country's life every day.

Per Albin regards himself as a good Marxist, a practical
Marxist. It is his conviction that the Social-Democratic line has
not deviated substantially since the formation of the party in
1889. There have been changes, of course, but not basic changes.
He recalls a speech made by Hjalmar Branting, the first labor
Prime Minister, in 1886; that same speech could be made today
and it would describe the policy the government is following.

In Per Albin's cabinet there is little faith in the prosperity of
recent years. If the long-threatening war does not finally break
and bring with it a crisis, then the new depression that has struck

America and, to a lesser degree, Great Britain will certainly make itself felt in Sweden. In anticipation of an almost inevitable downswing, the government is preparing detailed plans for public works that could be initiated very rapidly in the face of growing needs. The unemployed could be put to work, under these plans, within a few days after they had been certified as eligible. Not only is there a first line of defense but preparations are being made to meet a depression of even greater severity than that of 1933.

There are political observers who ascribe no small· share of the Laborites' success to Per Albin's abilities as a vote getter. He has a large personal following that extends into the middle class. And he is acutely conscious of the need for middle-class support. A certain antagonism toward organized labor and particularly toward building workers exists in Sweden. From anti-labor newspapers, and from other sources, too, one hears of the mythical "third party," the public in the role of innocent bystander in strikes and lockouts. As we have seen, one is told seriously that a man does not dare to paint his own house. Among professional people and small shopkeepers one can hear numerous stories of innocent victims of labor's drastic blockades and boycotts. This class is jealous of labor's solidarity and the power that comes from that solidarity.

In general, however, it would seem that there is very little rancor. This is not to say that the Right—the upper class, finance, and industry—did not make every effort possible to prevent the Socialist government from being returned to power. But once the election returns were in, they accepted the result calmly. The top men in finance and industry are rather inclined to the view that the whole structure of social services built up by the Left has been possible only because of the skill with which they, the Right, have organized industry, and especially export industry.

We in Sweden, they say, have rationalized our plants and our whole industrial process to a degree greater than in any other European country, unless it be Germany. We have brought unit production costs lower and lower and that is the reason why we can pay higher wages and sustain through taxation the burden of social services. And they argue that there is tangible evidence to support this view. They point to the fact that the wages of unionized workers in Sweden's wood-pulp industry are more than 35 per cent higher than the wages of nonunion workers in Finland. Yet the two countries compete in the same world market. (Actually, of course, the wood-pulp market is allocated between country and country by a kind of gentleman's agreement.) For contrast Swedish bankers and industrialists cite the example of France. One reason, and an important reason, why *l'expérience Blum* came to such an unfortunate end, they say, is because French industry has never been rationalized, brought up to an efficient level with wage scales correspondingly high.

About Per Albin there is something so solid and reassuring that it would be difficult to convert him into the traditional caricature of a Red. He is very fond of bridge, long motor trips, and bowling. And, a conscientious man, he works steadily and tirelessly at his job. Above all he recognizes his political responsibility as head of the party. Friends and admirers sought to prevail upon him to visit America at the time of the tercentenary celebration of the landing of the Swedes in Delaware. But there were municipal elections through the month of June and while they were not vital to the government's position, nevertheless Per Albin wanted the party to make a good showing.

What invariably astonishes the visitor from America is the almost total absence from the political scene of the kind of character assassination that we seem to take for granted. A man's private life, even though he hold public office, is his own. He may be living in sin or ten times divorced and if he is an honest and upright man, the general public will not know of it. At the start of their careers many of the young Laborites, in protest against the official church, declined to go through a marriage ceremony and simply set up housekeeping without benefit of ceremonial ties. This rather unusual circumstance has had no bearing on their political advancement.

The cabinet member whom businessmen fear, the bad man, is Wigforss, Minister of Finance. A former professor whose manner is still somewhat academic, Wigforss has a candor that is remarkable in a politician. The achievements of the government of which he is a part are in his view very limited, and they are due in no small measure to a fortuitous combination of circum-

Above: A performance of the Workers' Sport Association.

Below: Minister of Social Affairs for Sweden Gustaf Möller, Prime Minister Stauning, and Prime Minister Per Albin Hansson on the occasion of a visit to Copenhagen.

stances. With prosperity and a contracting national debt, his last budget message was extremely modest. Perhaps the most critical task today falls upon the Foreign Minister, Rickard Sandler.

In Sweden and in Norway, as in Denmark, it is the threat of war in northern Europe that disturbs the sleep of those who are responsible for government. Outwardly plans for the preservation of a joint neutrality are going forward. Privately there are grave doubts whether it will be possible in the next war to preserve any neutrality anywhere.

One complicating factor is the enormously rich store of iron in the north of Sweden. For more than thirty years Germany has been the principal customer for iron ore from the Kiruna mines. Next in line, but purchasing much smaller amounts, has been Great Britain. As the European armament race grew fiercer, however, the British looked about for new mineral resources. General Franco in Spain, at the instigation of Berlin, was limiting the exportation of Spanish ore to England. A new source of iron became an acute necessity for the British and they turned to Sweden.

They discovered the ancient relationship existing between the Swedish company that holds a monopoly on the right to exploit the northern mines and the Germans. Pressure was applied from Germany and the Grängesberg-Oxelösund Company told the British politely that it would be impossible to increase the amounts of ore then being sent to Great Britain. Promptly the British protested to the Swedish government, which by law controls the volume of ore to be taken out of the Kiruna mines and receives half of all the profits. Meanwhile Germany had hinted that any interference with the traditional arrangement whereby nearly 50 per cent of all German needs were supplied from the mines in Lapland might mean the permanent loss of Sweden's best customer.

However empty this threat may have been, it was an unpleasant moment for Sweden, caught between two hostile forces. The Swedes want to keep the peace with Germany if that is possible without loss of self-respect. A way out of the dilemma over the iron from Kiruna was found through a face-saving law allowing the company to increase the volume of ore taken each year from the mines. And so, for the time being at least, both sides of the great European divide were appeased.

But this can scarcely be regarded as a permanent solution and there must be times when, for all the wealth that they have brought, the Swedes wish that the great stores of iron had never been found in the north. The Germans have intimated that they would expect the line of ore boats which go from Luleå, on the Swedish coast, to Hamburg to continue even though a war should come that would involve the Baltic. Sweden is told in the official German naval journal that she has no use whatsoever for an army; let her spend her money for a navy and in time of war that navy can collaborate with the German fleet. This fits in perfectly with the views of high ranking Swedish naval officers who propagandize for a big navy very much after the fashion of naval officers all over the world.

Thus far this propaganda has not been markedly successful. While there has been extraordinary agreement among all classes and parties on the government's sizable budgetary increase for national defense, the advocates of a big navy have won few adherents. Elaborate preparations are being made to defend Stockholm from air raids. Coastal defenses up and down the whole rugged shore line are being strengthened.

There are certain very active pro-German influences in Sweden. Two newspapers, *Stockholms-Tidningen* and *Aftonbladet,* owned by the mysterious Torsten Kreuger, brother of the late Ivar Kreuger, are constantly advocating Germany's cause. The Swedish Foreign Office keeps a watchful eye on rumors and opinions appearing in these two dailies. Then, too, there are certain industrialists, although their number seems to be small, who look with a kind of envy on the freedom from labor trouble enjoyed by businessmen in Germany.

Serious-minded Swedes are concerned over the fact that Stockholm dailies are passing into the hands of wealthy men who tend to employ them as a means for expressing personal beliefs and prejudices. One of these rich men is Axel Wenner-Gren who left Sweden as a poor boy and returned with a fortune made in North and South America. Wenner-Gren owns *Nya Dagligt Allahanda,* a sensational Stockholm daily of tabloid size.

About Axel Wenner-Gren's success story there is something a little fabulous. With the fortune he got from the manufacture of patented household appliances he returned to make himself a power in his native land. He came back in time to buy at auction block prices some of the ruins of Ivar Kreuger's financial empire, particularly a huge holding of wood-pulp timber in the north. Then when the government discovered, with resulting shock and indignation, that a controlling interest in the great Bofors munitions works was held by Krupp of Germany through certain dummy directors, Axel Wenner-Gren again stepped in and bought out the German interest. This was after Parliament had passed a law forbidding foreigners to own the stock.

As with the Lapland mines, the European arms race has aroused intense interest in the output of the Bofors works, ranked by many military observers as the foremost munitions plant in the world. The orders at Bofors increased from $6,000,-000 in 1933 to $18,000,000 at the end of 1935, $27,250,000 by 1936 and $37,500,000 in 1937, with capacity production contracted for three years in advance. It was in February, 1936, that Bofors presented to the Swedish Navy the forty-millimeter automatic anti-aircraft gun, surpassing anything that had been hitherto developed for protection from raiding planes.

This gun became the immediate object of intense interest by all the powers. Early in 1937 the Bofors Company turned down a large order from Britain for the new anti-aircraft guns. The German connection was still strong even though, financially, there had been an official separation. But the British persisted, realizing that the new type of gun would be the best possible defense for London, and six months later Bofors accepted a $7,500,000 order with more important contracts to be let later.

In the present armament madness there is little that is consistent or rational. Alfred Nobel bequeathed his profits from the explosives industry to a fund from which awards for peace and the arts of peace are made. Similarly Axel Wenner-Gren in 1937 set aside about $7,000,000 to finance scientists, economists, and sociologists in their exploration of the ills that beset humanity. For his gift Wenner-Gren and his wife were decorated by King Gustaf with the order of the North Star. The workers at Bofors are more strongly pacifist than any other group in Sweden, it is said, just as the miners at Kiruna, which supplies Germany with half of her iron ore, have given more proportionately to the Spanish government than workers anywhere.

The war that is feared in Scandinavia is a war between Germany and Russia. The Russians in the event of such a war would not allow the ore boats to continue to go from Luleå to Hamburg. Sweden, and perhaps Norway, too, would find it all but impossible to remain neutral. Weird rumors of Russian airplanes spying in the north are given circulation in the sensational Stockholm newspapers. Scarcely a winter passes without a spy scare out of the Arctic Circle. These alarms, which seem to have very little basis in truth, are indicative of the forces beneath the surface that are making for war.

When they talk of neutrality in Scandinavia, they are aware of what the cost may be. During the World War Norway lost more than two thousand seamen on Norwegian vessels sunk by mines or submarines. When Dr. Halvdan Koht, the Norwegian Foreign Minister, discusses neutrality it is in terms of inevitable sacrifices, sacrifices far greater than those called forth by the last war. Norway, Dr. Koht insists, could, with the coöperation of the other Scandinavian countries, exist for a considerable period of time without imports. But rubber, oil, gasoline? We could keep a certain number of motor cars in service with illuminating gas, says Dr. Koht. It was what we did in 1917 and 1918. Life would be hard, it would be a struggle, but it would be possible to live.

The labor government of Norway is embarked on an extremely interesting experiment. While the Social-Democrats have retained some of the old forms, symbols, and shibboleths, they have put behind them the revolutionary past. They do not like to be reminded of this, seeking by a kind of rationalization to avoid the full implications of the new course they have chosen to follow. But nevertheless it is true.

Party leaders in Norway were convinced that the disaster to labor in Germany and Austria came about through the failure of the Left to realize what were the realities outside the closed sphere of Socialist and Marxist dogma. They decided that the process of socialization should not wait upon an arbitrary formula. In convention in 1933 the party voted to enter the forthcoming election campaign under the slogan: Labor majority and labor government. In 1935 the Socialists obtained sufficient votes to enable them to form a minority government which has remained in office ever since, collaborating alternately with the Farmer and the Liberal parties.

Under the guidance of such men as Johan Nygaardsvold, Prime Minister, the brilliant Martin Tranmael, editor of *Arbeiderbladet,* and Ole Colbjörnsen, economic adviser to the party, a very interesting policy has been evolved. It is based on the conviction that labor's first task, if the party is to remain in power and effect any significant changes, is to win over the middle class. The middle class must be convinced that its advantage lies with labor. This was the mistake that German and Austrian Socialists made. They thought in terms of the proletariat, narrowly defined, a trade-union monopoly, ignoring middle-class low income groups, white-collar workers, and farmers, who had far less than the official proletariat. It is not enough merely to fight for higher trade-union wages. We must consider the whole economy and our place in that economy, Norwegian Laborites argued. Benefits must go to farmers and fishermen—the middle class in Norway—even though in the beginning this may mean sacrifices by labor.

The national economy, at the outset at least, will be neither capitalist nor socialist.

The important thing [in the words of Finn Moe, foreign editor of *Arbeiderbladet*] is to make the "socialized sector" so strong that it can dominate the "private sector." The plan is to let the government get complete control of the whole banking and credit system, including the insurance companies. The most important branches of large-scale industry and some of the great forests will be socialized. The export and import trade will be made government monopolies. For the rest of the economic life, government regulation and control are considered sufficient.

At the start Norway's labor government has been concerned not so much with the long-time program as with improving the status of various classes and groups. But in order to raise standards of living it is necessary, in the view of Norwegian Labor party leaders, to expand the national economy. Again they look abroad for an example of what not to do. Léon Blum, in the view of Norwegian Laborites, attempted to pass out higher wages and government benefits in a static economy; it simply could not be done: inevitably Blum fell in the summer of 1937.

Therefore in Norway labor is subsidizing private industry, seeking to establish some measure of control in return for loans. A government controlled industrial bank has been created to finance the development of industries, and particularly industries in new fields. New factories have been financed with government funds for the manufacture of rayon from wood pulp. Large sums have been advanced to leading shipbuilding firms in order that the industry may be modernized. This coincides, of course, with a phase in the industrialization of a country which up until thirty years ago was almost entirely rural. Wherever it is possible, foreign capital is being retired. And foreign investors who formerly found an outlet for surplus money in the development of Norwegian industry, now discover that their capital is not wanted. With the aid of a labor government Norway's own industrialists are acquiring the industries initiated by foreigners.

For fishermen the government has guaranteed a minimum price on cod. And in addition large subsidies have been advanced to enable individual fishermen to free themselves of debt and buy new equipment. The bureau of fisheries has been enlarged so that it can give greater aid to the entire industry. Municipalities throughout the country have received generous subsidies and substantial loans from the labor government. This money has gone in considerable part to retire indebtedness incurred through the overexpansion of municipal power plants during the war. With the burden of debt reduced, municipalities have been able to divert more funds to those social services —such as free medical care and hospitalization—which are financed by local communities.

Benefits have been handed out directly through national legislation. At the insistence of the labor majority Parliament passed an old-age insurance act guaranteeing pensions to the needy aged. New state insurance laws covering the crippled and the blind have been adopted. The labor government is determined, too, to put through an unemployment insurance law. At present the unemployed receive aid from local communities under an ancient Poor Law Act.

All this, it is scarcely necessary to add, has cost large sums of money. To meet the demands for a greatly increased national revenue the labor government adopted, of all things, a uniform 2 per cent sales tax. This naturally falls hardest on workers in the cities. But the workers should expect to carry the burden in the beginning, Socialist leaders argued in defense of this extraordinary step. Later, when the party has won over a comfortable majority of the voters, including a substantial section of the middle class, the tax burden can be shifted. Nevertheless the sales tax was difficult to accept, only the stubborn stand of the Farmers' party against any increase in the national debt forcing the Socialists at last to seek this way out.

Labor's bold policy in Norway risks certain hazards. To the casual visitor it seems that the Norwegian experiment parallels in a rather alarming way *l'expérience Blum*. Prices rose through 1937 with startling rapidity, approaching close to the 1928 level. One heard a great deal of grumbling among the middle class and particularly in professional groups. If the benefits passed out by the government were to be nullified by upward price trends, then this was merely another example of bootstrap economics.

But the enthusiasm of those who have formulated the new policy will allow of no doubts. Younger men particularly, party leaders such as Ole Colbjörnsen, are supremely confident that they will be able to avoid the pitfalls which have caused labor's downfall elsewhere in Europe.

Colbjörnsen is one of the most interesting men to come to leadership in Scandinavia. Of a family of hardy peasant farmers, he developed early a genius for mathematics and it was assumed, as he passed rapidly through the lower schools and the university, that he would eventually become a professor. Instead he turned his attention to politics and became a Communist at a time when the Labor party in Norway was affiliated to the Third International. While still very young, he was invited to go to Russia. There his rise was spectacular and in his late twenties he became commissar of the wood industry. Disagreeing over details of policy, especially in the international field, he left Russia and renounced politics forever. His unquestioned brilliance won him a position with private business not long after his return to his native land and in a comparatively short time he became the London agent of a large Norwegian firm, a position of no little importance.

Colbjörnsen could not, however, stay out of politics for long. Returning to Norway he was drawn into the effort to reshape the direction of the Social-Democratic party. Along with other leaders he had come under the influence of the Belgian Socialist, Henri De Man, whose critique of the doctrines of the neo-Marxists seemed to Colbjörnsen to make sense. De Man's *The Psychology of Socialism* has had considerable influence in Norway.

The new approach to socialism, in the view of such ardent younger men as Colbjörnsen, is far more realistic if only because it presumes a transition period in which the middle class is converted—not by words so much as by a demonstration of labor's good intentions—to the need for drastic changes in the economy. Speaking in rapid English with scarcely a trace of accent, this earnest young Norwegian dissects the past and looks forward hopefully to the future.

With the British Labor party he is impatient, having known many of the leaders at first hand as a result of his stay in England. They sought to redistribute existing income, assuming that the capitalists would provide income for redistribution; failing to realize that they would come up against an economic crisis in which there would be no income to parcel out. As a result British labor received a blow from which it will not recover for many years. By contrast in Norway the effort has been to stimulate new production and put the unemployed back to work. And already the new policy is proving successful; there has been a real increase in the income of the working class and it has been derived almost entirely from an increase in the number of workers employed. The financial position of Norway, Colbjörnsen says, has not been so fortunate since the war.

Recently Colbjörnsen has been less influential. A dominating force today is Martin Tranmael who is certainly no less brilliant. Tranmael acquired a Syndicalist background in the course of several years of experience with the I.W.W. in America before the World War. But his Syndicalism was somewhat tempered on his return to Norway by a realization of the need to work, at least in a transition phase, through parliamentary methods. He was the chief advocate of industrial unionism and it was largely as a result of his influence that the trade-union movement was reorganized along industrial lines. This process, it may be added, has not yet been completed and at least two of the old craft unions have left the National Federation rather than accept the industrial principle. As editor he has made the *Arbeiderbladet* the most effective and popular labor daily in Scandinavia.

Tranmael has been an important force, too, in international labor politics. It was in large part as a result of his activity that the International Federation of Trade Unions made up its differences with Moscow and accepted the Soviet unions as affiliates.

There are skeptics, it might be added, who are doubtful of the new headlong policy. And they include some of the older and more conservative men within the government. These older leaders, including Prime Minister Nygaardsvold himself, have taken the public positions, allowing the younger men to formulate policy behind the scenes. But occasionally caution and timidity have prevailed in the party councils.

Then too, there is a militant rank and file who have shown their disapproval of certain phases of the present policy. Now and then the new strategy has for the militants the appearance of a retreat from the revolutionary principles of the past. And they insist that they have never given their sanction to any such about face. In short, they must be educated up to the subtleties of the new policy. But even education does not always prevail. At the party congress in 1934 the rank and file swept out all the leaders by means of a resolution condemning everyone who participated in a political bargain with the bourgeois parties over modification of certain laws. There is in this rank and file a vitality and a vigor, a kind of fierceness and independence, that owes not a little to the Norsemen of old. Distinct problems in discipline arise from time to time and the leaders talk privately of the need for compulsory wage agreements, enforced by precedent rather than by law, if their planned economy is to go according to the blueprint.

For the present the Social-Democrats are unquestionably in the ascendancy. On the extreme Left the Communists have dwindled in numbers to less than 5,000 and it is understood that Moscow has approved a merger with the Labor party. Relations with the Farmers' party, at one time extremely conservative and antilabor, have steadily improved. There is every external evidence that the new policy of coöperation is producing the results it was intended to produce.

The overwhelming task is to chart the course of the national economy in a world torn by war and the threat of war. The Scandinavian countries have in recent years drawn away from the League of Nations and the reason is not hard to find. In Norway, for example, the government carried out sanctions against Italy during the Ethiopian War in all earnestness. The result was the loss of a large part of the fisheries trade, a serious blow financially. And in the final showdown England pulled out so that the whole effort was no more than an empty bluff.

In Sweden and Norway they have come to feel that "collective security" is an illusion and a dangerous illusion. As the dictators have successfully defied the League Powers again and again, the Scandinavian powers have been more or less driven into a coöperative neutrality. The Swedes have accumulated large stores of essential commodities that must come from abroad. Bought with public funds, these commodities have been used as the base for the issuance of currency in a bold monetary experiment. In an important speech on foreign policy Foreign Minister Sandler quoted the following Belgian formula:

We are determined to make the strongest possible resistance against every attempt to violate our territory. We have done what we could to get the means for commanding respect. Outside the League of Nations we are not tied to anyone, but it goes without saying that we intend to treat all our neighbors with loyalty, understanding, and good will without reservation. What part of this definition of neutrality [Sandler asked his audience] does not apply to Sweden?

The sternest efforts are being made to preserve every appearance of neutrality. While it is true that public opinion is largely on the side of the Loyalist government in Spain and substantial sums have been raised for hospitals and the relief of the civilian population, the recruiting of soldiers for the war is forbidden. Communist recruiting centers have been broken up by the police. Recruiting is against the policy of nonintervention to which Sweden subscribed. And the Swedes believe in obeying the letter of the law.

In the summer of 1937 the suggestion that the Scandinavian peninsula might be devastated as the Iberian peninsula at the other extreme of Europe has been destroyed by foreign invaders was regarded as too ludicrous even for consideration. It was beyond the bounds of possibility since it implied an historical background that would provide the excuse for the invasion. It could not happen in Sweden. That sums up the attitude of men and women on the Right and on the Left. And certainly it would seem from all circumstances, past and present, that that kind of civil-foreign war could scarcely occur in Scandinavia.

But the way in which the Nazis absorbed Austria was something else. This was nearer at hand, it involved a small and distracted people. True there was the racial kinship. But why could not the same thing happen in that area of mixed population awarded to Denmark at the close of the World War? It was a frightening object lesson close at hand of the ruthless resort to force of an absolute dictatorship.

One reason why Sweden and Norway have drawn away from the continent in what amounts almost to a defensive alliance is the deadly paralysis that has come upon British foreign policy. Ever since the defeat of the pro-German party centering around the Queen and the court during the World War, Sweden, and Norway too, have looked to Great Britain for leadership of a sort. In recent years they have seen Britain vacillate painfully and awkwardly, doing nothing and doing it very badly. From this quarter there has been no guidance, no support whatsoever.

Primarily, however, the desire for neutrality comes out of a profound realization of the cost of war. Neutrality means, as these countries in the north know very well, tremendous sacrifices, an adjustment of the entire economy. But the cost is nothing as compared to the cost of war. There is here in the north no fearful burden of war debt and that, the Scandinavians know, too, is one reason, an important reason, why they have been able to establish a decent social order and a large measure of peace in the chaos of postwar Europe.

CHAPTER V

THE FARMER AND THE WORKER

FROM the superficial view there is every reason why city workers and farmers should unite politically. Their interests, as producers, would appear to be the same. Nor, if one simplifies the problem a little, does there appear any essential economic barrier to an amicable relationship between these two groups; beneath all the complexities of modern society the exchange between the farmer and the artisan is still at the base of our economy.

Yet in almost every country in the world in recent decades a bitter opposition between farmer and factory worker, city and country, has come into being. Shrewd politicians have capitalized on this opposition, realizing that it is to the interest of the owning class to foment such a division. The small landowners were an important factor in Hitler's rise to power in Germany. Opposition of the peasants threatened for a time to disrupt the Soviet Union and the internecine warfare that followed was ended by a famine of ghastly proportions. In our own Congress a favorite theme is the failure of Senators and Representatives from rural areas to support labor legislation.

The politicians, it is obvious, have not created this split. They merely exploit it. Here, it would seem, is one of the profound maladies from which the present-day world is suffering. And somehow a cure must be found if representative government is to survive. In the northern democracies it is possible to look at this problem without too many complicating factors, with a kind of laboratory detachment. Partly this is because they are small countries with a homogeneous population. But more important is the fact that in Scandinavia there is a deep awareness of the seriousness of the problem and the urgent need for a solution. It is felt by some acute observers in the north that the future of Western civilization may turn on the possibility of resolving the deep opposition between the townsman and the countryman.

The Danes in this respect are in a particularly difficult situation. Farming is the principal industry, and, moreover, farming for export. Even with the best of intentions toward this mainstay of the whole economy, the labor government obviously could not follow the course taken by other countries in recent years. In Sweden and Norway they have guaranteed a domestic price level to the farmer for his principal commodities and a subsidy is paid to him on the excess production that is sent abroad to make up the difference between the world price and the domestic price. But it would be plainly impossible to subsidize the thousands of tons of Danish butter—a large part of the total production—that go into world trade.

The Danish farmers insist nevertheless that they must have a larger share of the national income. They are profoundly dissatisfied and their dissatisfaction has in recent years taken a rather ominous form. It has the look, this revolt of the farmers, of an incipient Fascist movement.

In part it has its origins in the peculiar economic organization of farming in Denmark. Fertilizer and fodder must be imported, under the present system, from abroad. America and the Orient are the chief sources of the raw materials that go into Denmark's farm industry. The necessity to import the stuff to feed Danish dairy herds and to fertilize intensely cultivated fields puts agricultural production—for profit on the world market—under a severe handicap. As we have seen the Danish farmer must buy his raw material at a comparatively high price and then he must send his finished product across tariff barriers and against quota restrictions at a relatively low price.

No wonder then that there is widespread discontent among the checkerboard farms that are so efficiently and carefully managed, so neat, so trim. There are experts in the government who believe that it might be possible to change the system of Danish farming in such a way that the farmer would no longer be dependent upon imports. This could be done, it is argued, through the use of silos and the cultivation of a silage crop that would supply the same elements for winter fodder as now come from American cotton seed. No real effort has been made, these same experts say, to change the base of the farming industry. Any serious effort in that direction would, of course, come up against old traditions and prejudices. And it sometimes seems that farmers, more than any other class in the world, are bound to tradition, bound by what has gone before.

There is another and perhaps even more important source of the discontent that pervades the Danish farm population. And here particularly one can observe the symptoms of a malady from which every country in the world is suffering. It is the malady of debt. During the World War there was a heavy demand for Danish farm products. At that time cattle were slaughtered as never before, cattle that actually represented a part of the capital of Danish dairy farmers. Then in the brief boom that followed the war, farmers went heavily into debt to restock their farms. And this burden of debt was built upon the boom time valuation of farm land, an unreasonable valuation.

What has happened in Denmark has happened all over the world. Excessive values have been forced down but not sufficiently, for the money value put upon land is still far too high. In the worst years of the world depression it was impossible for the farmer to earn any return whatsoever on his land. In a large number of instances loans exceed the present valuation of the farms on which they were made. In 1932 the average return was equivalent to about 4 per cent on all Danish farms. While this was zero in 1933, it had returned to approximately 3 per cent in 1936. Again in 1937, however, the percentage return began to fall, as world commodity prices receded. Common sense plainly indicates a revision downward of land values. But what happens to that towering structure of debt when values are forced down to rational levels? It is a kind of tottering tower of Babel and under its long uncertain shadow we have all lived in the postwar years.

Various methods have been resorted to to scale down the debt structure in the Scandinavian countries but they have not been drastic enough; methods similar to those tried in other parts of the world, moratoriums and reduction of the interest rate. The Danish farmer must go on making his payments because his mortgage, and thousands upon thousands of others like it, is somewhere at the base of the financial heap and what may happen if the whole thing is upset no one dares to think. But as he pays he grumbles and in his discontent he is ready to follow the first man who talks loud enough and long enough.

And inevitably an organization came into being to give mass expression to the unrest prevailing on Danish farms. This Farm-Workers' Association—Landbrugernes Sammenslutning, usually shortened to L.S.—organized the great march on Copenhagen that took place just before the harvest in the summer of 1935. Carefully prepared weeks in advance, the demonstration drew thousands upon thousands of small farm owners to the capital for a direct appeal to King Christian X. They converged upon Amalienborg Palace, an orderly but nevertheless irresistible stream of humanity, until they entirely filled the great square before the handsome eighteenth-century façade. At last in response to the cries of the crowd the King, the Crown Prince, and other members of the royal family came out onto the central balcony. It was a setting that Hollywood might have envied; the tall figure of the King, seemingly impervious to the roar of sound that swept up from the packed mass of humanity, the fringes of the crowd extending even into connecting streets, red and white flags held high above the throng.

The picturesque aspects of the demonstration in Amalienborg Square were lost upon the Laborites; its implications were too serious. The march itself was illegal, the Socialists said, a charge hotly denied by the farmers. Was not the King the head of the state, they demanded? Therefore they had a perfect right to present their grievances to him. What was more, said the Socialists, the Nazis were behind the formation of L.S. As one proof, *Social-Demokraten* in Copenhagen printed a photograph of an L.S. leader giving what was said in the caption to be the Nazi salute. This charge, too, the farmers denied in the pages of their own journal; the photograph they pronounced a fake. The quarrel between the two factions at the time of the Amalienborg march was extremely bitter. As a result of the march the government granted a temporary respite on indebtedness which enabled thousands of farmers to hang on until the harvest was in.

Two large landowners were at that time the real leaders of the organization. While Count Knuth and Hofjaegermester Sehested have since become less active, they supplied initiative

Above: The Square before Amalienborg Palace crowded with farm demonstrators demanding farm legislation.

Below: May Day demonstration by trade unions and Labor party in Stockholm.

and money to start the movement in the first instance. The land holdings of most of the members are, of course, small. More than half of all farms in Denmark are under twenty-five acres and scarcely more than 10 per cent have as many as seventy-five acres.

Like most organizations of its kind, the program of the Danish farmers' association is very vague. The chief objective is a "proper price" for agricultural products. To achieve this L.S. has suggested that a tax be imposed on valuta, or import, permits. Such permits must be obtained for any import, regardless of size, and the government through this form of valuta control has in recent years maintained a strict check on what has been brought into the country. Under the tax proposed by the farmers it would be necessary to pay heavily for the privilege of importing certain kinds of goods, particularly luxury goods. The revenue derived in this way would go—you've guessed it—to subsidize farm exports.

Behind the avowed program of L.S. is an underlying hostility toward the workers in the city. Trade-union wages, the farmer feels, are too high. Those who have larger holdings and employ help belong for the most part to the Venstre party which has been in almost constant opposition to the labor government. The official Venstre paper is extremely reactionary, opposing social insurance of every kind out of the conviction that city workers prefer idleness under an insurance-dole scheme to work. Farmers with small holdings, roughly one half of the 200,000 farm families, are Radical-Lefts. The votes of this party in Parliament have kept the Laborites in power.

They have also been responsible, in the opinion of objective critics, for the timidity and caution of the present government. There has been, it must be repeated, no substantial reduction in the burden of farm debt. "They are too worshipful of the credit agencies and the insurance companies." That is the judgment of a good many young intellectuals who would push the Social-Democrats to the Left.

Over a number of years a serious effort has been made to unionize farm laborers. Formation of a special organization in each parish, around which the union should be built, was attempted. But there have been numerous obstacles and it is doubtful if more than 35,000 of the 80,000 employed farm laborers have ever been organized. Working on Danish farms are at least 100,000 sons, daughters, and other members of farm families and they, of course, can never be brought into any kind of organization. Then there has been a constant shift of workers from the country to the city which has made for instability. Another problem is that of child labor. In Jutland children of twelve may be employed through the summer. The laws vary from province to province but it is taken for granted that after confirmation at fourteen children will go to work. Frequently they are employed from fourteen to nineteen and then dismissed by farmers seeking cheaper help.

All these factors have worked against unionization. A separate trade union for farm workers was established in 1915; up until that time they had been merely affiliated to the central organization. In 1934 the Farm-Workers' Union became part of the General Workers' Union which is made up of the unskilled, divided among transport, the building industry, factory, agriculture, and forestry. The unemployment insurance law has served somewhat to stimulate organization on the farms but no one appears to be hopeful that any substantial number of farm workers will be brought within the trade-union fold.

In periods of prosperity, or comparative prosperity, the grumble of discontent from the farms subsides. But nothing has been solved and it will be heard again. In the event of another world-wide depression, with commodity prices slipping lower and lower, it seems certain that the farmers would march again. And their march might not be so peaceful another time. Sweeping out the labor government, they might sweep out with it the system of benefits and reforms that has been so painstakingly built up over a long period of years.

While the whole farm problem is far less acute in Sweden, it nevertheless exists. There, too, they realize the need to resolve the underlying differences between rural and urban populations. They talk in terms of the need for a fundamental change in the system of land ownership. Looking back to first causes, they see what a profound alteration was worked by the *code Napoléon*. It completely disrupted the forms of collective ownership that had prevailed in part at least even through the eighteenth century. Granted outright ownership of the land and the right to pass it on to his heirs, the European peasant was beset with the ambition to increase his holdings so that each heir might have a portion of land, or so that the oldest son might inherit an impressive tract. All the virtues inherent in group ownership—a common concern for the well-being of the whole community which went along with a regard for the fertility of the soil—were immediately swept aside.

In Sweden they have begun to discuss what may be at least an approach to a long-time solution. What is the real result, they have demanded, of the agricultural policy of the past decade? The government has provided export subsidies on certain major commodities, which means that the consumer has been paying the farmer the difference between a domestic price, sustained by government guarantees and import restrictions, and the world price. In other words the consumer pays a tax to the farmer on that share of the farmer's production which is presumably a surplus—beyond the volume that can be consumed within the country. It is this same assumption, of an exportable surplus beyond the needs of the population, that is at the bottom of subsidy schemes throughout the world.

The Swedish subsidy scheme, even considering the scale of agricultural production, has been comparatively modest. In 1937 the government was prepared to pay out between 10 and 20,000,000 crowns as an export subsidy for butter. The revenue for this was derived from a tax on cheaper competing fats, particularly margarine which is a staple in poorer households. Another 5,000,000 was available to underwrite exports of bacon and eggs. But the total would not go above 25,000,000. In addition the government since 1931 has bought grain for storage to the amount of about 90,000,000, this being a part of the program to guarantee a domestic price level.

The alliance of Socialists with farmers in the government has depended in no small degree, of course, on state aid to agriculture. But within the Socialist party there were those who realized that the export subsidy system was at best a stop-gap. While it has served undoubtedly to sustain farm purchasing power, it has put a definite penalty on families with low incomes not only in the cities but in rural areas as well. Nevertheless there it was, an integral part of the political structure that maintained the Socialists in power. How to change it? How to alter political values without alienating farm support?

The approach to this problem has been worked out by such brilliant younger members of the party as Professor Gunnar Myrdal and his wife, Alva Myrdal. First of all they sought to raise certain major doubts. Is this surplus that we endow for export really a surplus? Does it represent so much butter, eggs, bacon, grain beyond the needs of every last Swedish citizen? No one could give an unqualified answer to these large and somewhat embarrassing questions. All right then, said the questioners, let's find out the answers. Let's not base our policy on a mere assumption that may be right or wrong.

Out of this discussion came the appointment by the government of the Population Commission, authorized to look into every phase of the Swedish standard of living. Some twenty leaders representing all departments of life were named to the commission and leading scientists and economists were delegated to carry out the studies.

Two book-length reports have already come from the commission. The first of these reports was *The Sexual Question* and the second was *Dietary Standards.* It is the conviction of those who have been really responsible for the work of the commission that no country in the world has ever attempted so objective an examination of all the factors and forces that make up a way of life. The two reports already completed are ample proof of this, it seems to me. I do not know of any country outside of Scandinavia in which such a high degree of scientific detachment would be possible. All too often elsewhere the ruling class has decreed a living standard that is an empty fiction; any realistic examination of the facts is impossible. Instead of scientific examination of reality there is propaganda to convince the masses that they must be well off.

A large part of *The Sexual Question* is taken up with an analysis of the reasons for Sweden's low birth rate, one of the lowest in the world. The authors consider economic factors; the social and economic penalties that go with many children. But they consider, too, all the implications of birth restriction in modern society. Not only is the sexual impulse analyzed from the medical and social point of view but the emotional phase of human reproduction is examined in relation to the impact of machine civilization.

One section of the report is devoted to the fight against venereal diseases as it affects the birth rate. There are in Sweden four active cases of syphilis for each one hundred thousand persons in contrast to the United States where there are nine hundred cases for each one hundred thousand of population. The need to remedy the basic economic causes of the spread of infection is stressed throughout. An example of the thorough-going nature of the whole study is seen in the remarks in this section about the relationship between housing and the commonest source of venereal infection, which is prostitution. Overcrowding, in that it almost invariably results in sexual precocity, contributes to a psychic predisposition to prostitution.

"These sexual experiences," the report says of the conditions that prevail in overcrowded homes, "are in many instances of a character shocking to children and are not infrequently of an incestuous nature. This impersonal sexual behavior readily becomes the pattern of conduct. It cramps the development of the young, particularly with regard to the need for completion and psychic individualization in the love life." I submit that that is a remarkable passage to come from a government report signed by leaders of the community including a bishop of the church.

A tone of high seriousness marks the entire report. Weighing the results of the widespread use of birth control, the commission found that the trend toward a "rationalization" of the sex life had brought effects "which must be judged as good in themselves." These good effects are briefly summed up. "But on the other hand," the commission adds, "many inquire anxiously whether a nation will be able to survive if the production of children is generally subjected to the control of intelligent deliberation. In so far as we value our nation's continued existence, we must, should this anxiety be warranted, judge birth control to be harmful—yes, in the most real sense, dangerous to life. This being the circumstance no citizen can consider himself exempt from forming an opinion. In our effort to create, through wisdom, industry and sacrifice, a better community in the future, we all count on our nation's continuing to live. Our efforts would otherwise, except for the narrowly egotistical point of view, be wasted." But the fact of the widespread prevalence of birth control must be faced, the report continues, and future policy based upon a recognition of the reality. One is tempted to quote again and again from this extraordinary document.

In a sense these findings were incidental to the real work of the commission which was to show the living standards that prevail at various income levels. In a lengthy appendix to *The Sexual Question* the economist Rickard Sterner analyzes living standards in relation to average income. And the second report is devoted almost entirely to an analysis of dietary standards.

The picture presented is not at all flattering to the ego of the average Swede, proud of the progressiveness of his country. It was found that there were wide areas of malnutrition, particularly in the rural districts of the north. Shockingly low incomes of farm and forest workers were brought to light. Even in the cities it was found that a large number of workers have incomes so low that minimum standards of decency can scarcely be maintained. Striking differences were shown between families with one or two children and families with many children. The latter consumed fifteen pounds of butter per person each year while the former used twice as much, on the same income level. And in the consumption of milk, eggs, and fresh vegetables the same disproportion prevailed.

Despite a program of coöperative and public housing extending over a number of years, widespread overcrowding was found by the commission. Here particularly it was shown that the large family is penalized. Nearly half of all city dwellings were found to consist of one room and kitchen. The conclusion was inescapable that not only small households but at least 40 per cent of all families with three or more children occupied such flats. And on the lower income levels not less than half of all families with several children lived in one room and kitchen.

Perhaps the only real gain in housing in the past two decades has come not through the construction of thousands of new low-cost apartments but through restriction on the size of families, the commission suggested. The present birth rate in Sweden is about 30 per cent below the minimum level required to maintain a stationary population. About one half of all households have only one child or none. Actually fewer than 5 per cent of all families in Stockholm have three children or more and less than 12 per cent of all families in the capital have two children. The commission found that if the population is to be kept stationary, it will be necessary for at least one half of the households with one child or none to have at least four children.

No sooner had the first report been presented than it became the subject of earnest discussion throughout the whole country. Speakers talked about it on the radio. Professor Myrdal reduced the principal findings to the scope of a pamphlet which sold thousands of copies. The national living standard became a sharp political issue. Through the summer of 1937 a parliamentary committee toured the rural districts in the north. Conservative members of the committee discovered that children had apple cheeks and looked healthy enough. Surely, they reported in interviews in the press, this talk about malnutrition must be exaggerated. And what of the fine schools and gymnasiums that we saw? There is no need to talk about housing when children can attend such fine schools. Why, when I was a child . . . But the facts contained in the commission's report could not be so easily faced down.

The foreign reaction to the commission's report was revealing. In the *Times* of London there appeared a long editorial expressing horror that such poverty should exist. The piously complacent tone of the *Times* annoyed certain of the experts and economists who had participated in the preparation of the report. Their comment was that if the English were to examine objectively living standards in the British Isles they would find far more reason to be shocked. Grinding poverty in Britain is taken for granted as the inevitable lot of the great mass of the population; a medical study published some years ago showed more than half of the entire population suffering from malnutrition. The fact is that no country in the world can afford to be smug about living standards today. When we in this country talk about the American standard of living, we conveniently ignore vast blighted areas such as the Appalachian Highlands and the Dust Bowl.

But to get back to the political strategy behind the work of the commission. The picture presented in the commission's report was not intended merely to shock and startle the Swedes out of their complacency. That was one motive, but strategists within the Labor party knew that a practical program of action must be put forward immediately since that kind of shock does not last for long. There had been a decided political gain in having the report presented by the commission and signed by national leaders; malnutrition, overcrowding, low wages, as testified to by such eminent authorities, surely could not be reduced to terms of mere partisanship.

And the program that was put forward had a similar virtue. If people are hungry, then feed them. Could there possibly be any political argument about that? The Socialists proposed to give free lunches to all public school children in Sweden. Not just to children in need of such feeding, for that would serve to put an undemocratic stigma on hunger, but to all children.

This [said Professor Myrdal] is how we shall use a large part of the farm "surplus." As the Population Commission has shown us, it is no surplus at all. The cost? Well, we paid about 25,000,000 crowns in 1937 as an export subsidy on a "surplus" that our own people were badly in need of. The commission has demonstrated that if families with three or more children consumed the average amount of foodstuffs, the income of Swedish farmers would be increased by more than 100,000,000 crowns. Let's as a start spend 30,000,000 to give free lunches in all public schools. That will more than replace the old subsidy and it will be paid by taxes just as before but by taxes that we hope will be more equitably distributed.

This, it should be emphasized, is only a start; a way out of the nightmare dilemma of scarcity in the midst of plenty. Above all it is an effort at political education, a practical demonstration of how economic values may be transposed to the good of a whole society. In this last respect particularly it is very impressive, a lesson that other states might well study.

In still another field the Social-Democrats have linked their farm subsidy scheme to the general welfare. This, in effect, was what they said to the farmers: If the government guarantees a fair price for your production and grants you a subsidy on your exportable surplus, then you must improve working conditions and wages of farm labor. And since your price and your subsidy are guaranteed by law, the farm laborer should also have some guarantee of law.

It was in 1936 that the labor government proposed a law limiting the hours of work of agricultural workers. A detailed schedule of hours was included in the law. Ordinary agricultural laborers would work forty-one hours a week during the months of December, January, and February, forty-six hours during March, October, and November, and fifty-four hours in the months from April through September; those having the care of animals nine hours in every twenty-four hours and no more than one hundred and eight hours every two weeks; and for workers in truck gardens a maximum of ten hours every twenty-four hours and ninety-six hours every two weeks. To these totals could be added overtime, at overtime rates, up to two hundred hours a year.

At the time that this reform was proposed the Social-Democrats lacked a working majority in Parliament. The proposal was taken up and passed by the bourgeois majority but in such a form that the resulting law was practically worthless. It had been amended to cover only farms and truck gardens employing at least five workers; persons having the care of animals were excluded entirely. Still the new law was of some benefit since it limited the total number of hours in a year to 2,600, which was about the limit that organized agricultural labor had succeeded in obtaining by wage contract.

But in the campaign of 1936 the Social-Democrats pointed to it as an example of middle-class treachery. It appeared on the surface to be a beautiful reform but it was not a reform at all since it applied to such a small number of individuals. Returning to power with a clear majority, the Laborites proceeded, in collaboration with the Farm party, to put over what was substantially their original proposal.

Basically, however, it was recognized from the beginning that any real improvement in the status of the farm laborer would have to come through his own collective efforts, through his own trade-union organization. Higher wages, security in his job, could not be conferred upon him by law. There had never been on the statute books in Sweden a law guaranteeing the right of collective bargaining; no such law had been necessary. But because of the peculiar difficulties confronting union leaders and organizers in the agricultural field, farm employers had in many districts resisted, and successfully, all attempts to organize. In 1936 a law forbidding any infringement on union rights was proposed and finally passed although in a form slightly altered from the original draft.

The Farm-Workers' Union received an immediate stimulus from the new law. There are now between 35,000 and 40,000 dues-paying members which compares with 19,000 at the end of 1935. Leaders are confident that within two years it will be possible to bring virtually all of the hundred thousand farm workers within the union. Five full-time organizers are in the field besides a number of ardent volunteers who do part-time work. In the months that have followed passage of the law the growth of the organization of farm employers has kept pace with that of the union. Plainly it will not be long before the machinery for collective bargaining on the farms is as firmly established as it is in industry.

The Farm-Workers' Union prosecutes strikes and "blockades," that is, boycotts, with all the vigor of an industrial union. There were ten local strikes in 1937, all of them resulting in gains for the union. The law requires that a week's notice be given by the union if a strike is to be called or by the employer if a lockout is contemplated. A government mediator makes every effort during this period to settle the dispute but if fundamental differences are still unresolved at the end of the week, a boycott is proclaimed. Notices are posted all around the farm calling on the public to abstain from buying any milk or other produce there and asking for general support. Workers who are directly concerned with the care of animals are not called out so that dairy herds and other livestock are tended to as usual. But if the employer should try to bring in strike-breakers, then every man and woman on the farm will go out. These strikes receive support from the central organization which pays benefits of a minimum of $4.50 a week to strikers. Affiliated to the General Federation of Trade Unions, the Farm-Workers' Union is an integral part of the Labor movement.

But for all the efforts of the union, and it has brought about real gains, there was a general recognition that farm wages were far too low. From various quarters proposals have come for raising standards by law. The Farmers' Association, which represents a number of farm employers, recommended that wages in agriculture be tied to an index of prices of agricultural products. It was argued that wages should rise and fall with that index but an investigation showed that such a method was impractical. And the Socialists insisted, too, that it was essentially unfair.

What the labor government proposed was that the minimum wage be fixed at the scale which the union should win through collective bargaining. Thus if the organized minority should win an increase in wages, a state authority could declare that the new wage level applied for all workers and all employers in agriculture. It was objected by some that under such a system the unorganized would have no incentive to join the union. But sponsors of the proposal could point to experience in England under minimum wages established by trade boards which showed exactly the opposite result. Union membership increased in trades where such boards were set up. Or at any rate this was true in certain trades and particularly in the earlier years of British experience under the Trade Boards Act, adopted in 1911. More recently, the effect of establishment of a Trade Board in a sweated industry, under the terms of the act, has seemed to be the opposite and British trade-union leaders have come to question the law. It is expected that the Farmer-Labor majority in Sweden will shortly put through Parliament a law fixing minimum wages for farm workers at trade-union levels.

Only a very few tenant farmers and owners of small holdings belong to the union. They have their own organization with a membership of about 160,000. It is in general a pressure group, the objective being higher prices for farm produce. But unlike the comparable organization in Denmark, its policy is not reactionary. Many of these small farmers work in the forests in the winter for wages.

For forest workers and migratory farmers the Socialist government has initiated a special program. An investigation showed that if they were able to settle on a small piece of land, producing food for their immediate household, their position was thereby immeasurably bettered. The program finally adopted by parliament was a modest one providing loans up to $1,500, in part a subsidy, in part bearing a low interest rate and amortizing over a period of thirty years. Between 1933 and 1936 nearly $10,000,000 went to acquire small holdings in this way, starting first in the provinces of Värmland and Dalarna, being extended later to the entire country. Payments under the plan can never be more than about $33 a year.

Per Edvin Sköld, Minister of Agriculture, said in a campaign speech in 1936 urging an extension of the program:

From every point of view it has been shown that confidence and social courage are restored to these people. I can give you an example. Recently I visited the small farm acquired by a forest worker. Formerly when the lumbering season was over he and his wife and their two children were forced from time to time to apply for poor relief. Now they live in a substantial house, most of which the man had built himself. In the barn were three cows and the land was under excellent cultivation. No one could say that he was unemployed during the summer. He had become a man who could stand on his own two feet. What he had gained in self-reliance and self-esteem cannot be estimated. What the family has gained in hope for the future can scarcely be measured. And the community has lessened the burden of relief by one family. This is one example. Gradually it will be multiplied many thousand times over.

In still another way the labor government has worked to raise standards of living on the farms. Each year a sum has been appropriated to subsidize the improvement of homes occupied by farm workers. More than 3,000 houses have been brought up to standard in this way with the expenditure of more than $1,000,000. The Socialists also proposed a law forbidding employers from evicting farm workers in the event of a strike for a period of three months but in its course through Parliament it was emasculated by the Conservative-Liberal majority which then prevailed and became as a consequence the subject for campaign recriminations.

There is not sufficient space to detail other phases of the far-reaching effort to strike a balance between the standards of farm and city, to reconcile the differences that set apart the farm hand and the industrial worker.

The problem in Norway is of another kind. There labor has been confronted with a Farm party openly hostile to the whole trade-union structure. The votes of farm representatives in Parliament put over the law forbidding boycotts, which meant the loss of a powerful weapon in a prolonged strike. The task of the Socialist government in Norway has been to win the good will of the farmers by direct and immediate benefits. This was the reason for the export subsidies granted by labor and financed through a sales tax. Later the time will come for a more carefully integrated program.

All this shows that a farmer-labor alliance can come only out of long, painstaking effort to bridge the hostility that is latent today. It cannot come out of wishing or philosophizing. There must be a tangible demonstration of the desire for a common standard; a desire to improve the living conditions of both rural and city workers. This is the only basis for a Labor-Farmer party that will endure. In Sweden they have begun to show the way for such an alliance, established on an understanding that has every appearance of being sound and permanent. It is an example of political acumen that other and far larger nations might profit from.

CHAPTER VI

LABOR GOES TO SCHOOL

IT would be difficult to imagine a more typically Swedish landscape than that at Brunnsvik in the province of Dalarna. Silver birches with their delicate, soft foliage stand along the shore of Lake Väsman, a placid body of water that is ringed in the farther distance with dark pines and spruces. There is in this landscape all the subtle tenderness that Swedish poets have so long celebrated. The setting is an ideal one for two institutions that embody a great deal of the essential spirit of the country and the people: the Brunnsvik People's College and the Swedish Trade-Union Federation School.

In the Swedish style, designed for simplicity and economy and painted the bold shade of red that is so characteristic, the buildings of the two schools are grouped along the shores of the lake. A green hill in the background rises steeply to an abandoned mine shaft. In the Federation School for three months, from the beginning of June through August, sixty young men and women from trade unions all over the country follow an intensive course of study that is intended to develop leadership.

They have been selected from a list made up by the local branch of the union to which they belong. The effort is always to get those young people who have been most active in the work of the union. The only arbitrary limitation is an educational prerequisite. To be eligible it is necessary to have had a six months' course at a folk high school such as the Brunnsvik People's College or equivalent training through the study courses of the Workers' Education Association. Needless to say there is sharp competition for admission to the school and a young person who misses the chance once will apply next year and the year after that. In the decade that it has existed many influential leaders have come out of Brunnsvik. They are brilliant young people who come here, the visitor is told with pride.

One cannot be at Brunnsvik for long without realizing that the formal instruction is only a part, and perhaps not the most important part, of what this school has to offer. Founded by Sigfrid Hansson, the school reflects his personality in so many ways that his retirement now after ten years of service raises a question as to the method to be followed in the future. Above all, as Mr. Hansson conceived it, the trade-union school was to be a forum for the free exchange of ideas; although forum is not the word since there was to be so little formalized activity outside the classroom.

Every subject under the sun comes up for discussion and debate sooner or later at Brunnsvik. Sitting about after lunch or supper, in free periods between classes, sun bathing on the shores of the lake, these young men and women talk over not only their own trade-union problems, but national and world politics and the impact of the ideologies that have sundered the European continent. Despite the peace and quiet of the setting, it is clear to the visitor that this is no mere bucolic retreat.

I know of no other school in the world that is quite like it. It may be the students. You could never mistake their seriousness of purpose, their eagerness, their keen intellectual curiosity. And yet, this is an outing, a kind of summer such as most of them have never known before, and they are determined to make the most of that too. And since they represent every region, a great many industries, and all shades of political opinion, the summer is hardly long enough to say all that has to be said.

To understand the part that Mr. Hansson has played in the creation of this institution it is important to see him in the midst of it. A portly figure in tweed golf knickers, he strolls like a good-humored pope along the neat gravel walks, a kind of Kris Kringle twinkle in his eyes that even horn-rim spectacles cannot conceal. At the outset of each term he has announced that for his part he will use the intimate form, the "du," and he hopes that this will meet with the same response. As he passes along, he stops to exchange a word here and there, a joking reference usually. If the formal address is used, he is very likely to say, "What's the matter? Are you annoyed with me today?" And from him this does not seem forced.

Finding a group of students on the steps of the dormitory, he is apt to stop and take part in the conversation. Very often these discussions turn on the course of Sweden's own trade-union movement and more likely than not one of the group will challenge Mr. Hansson's point of view. There is nothing that he enjoys more than the give and take of these arguments.

Here is a young man from one of the mining areas in the north, twenty-four years old, a Communist. Whoever may have started the argument, it is not long before this young man Olson and Mr. Hansson are in the midst of a warm debate, good-natured but very, very serious. The director comes back again and again to the need for an industrial discipline. What, he demands, is to take the place of the discipline of ownership, of management? It is not enough to talk in ideological terms since the question is one of techniques and practical controls. The Marxian thesis? Why the Marxian thesis has been invalidated by modern technology. And it is nonsense to talk about the redistribution of wealth in the face of mass production. Moreover, he adds, Swedish workers are not in favor of the socialization of all industry. To prove this last he cites the answers to a questionnaire distributed among 5,000 steel workers at Sandviken; they were for socialization in principle but opposed to socialization of the Sandviken works where they were employed.

To all of this, and part of it of course has been merely argumentation, Olson replies. You represent, he says, the reformist trade-union movement and that movement has definite achievements to its credit. But consider it from the longer view. What has it done? Above all it has resulted in the blurring of class lines. And therefore it can never have any real effect on the capitalist system; ameliorative, perhaps, in a small degree, but never touching those fatal defects inherent in the system itself. Nor can it ever succeed in greatly enlarging the workers' share of the national income. Isn't it possible that we have begun already to be aware of its final limitations? Young Olson is always respectful but he doesn't hesitate to carry the war into the enemy's camp.

Such an argument is never resolved, of course. With a final good-natured fling Mr. Hansson goes on his way. As likely as not the group will continue the talk after the director has

Above: A party around a provincial special dish, "Syrströmming," at Brunnsvik.

Below: Trade-union representatives from nine countries discuss current problems at Brunnsvik.

passed on. There is the impression that many of these young people, and particularly the more serious among them, are engaged in a somewhat skeptical examination of the trade-union movement in Scandinavia. They do not expect, one gathers, very many easy victories in the future.

The insistence upon facts and proof that ran through this argument is characteristic of the whole school. Before you argue political and economic theory, you must know your facts. That is a primary rule at Brunnsvik. Students often challenge teachers on fact and it is a favorite classroom device for sending hotheaded theorists to reference books and statistical analyses. If you advocate socialization and hold up Russia as an example, then you must know a great deal about production indexes and the status of industry before 1917 and after. If you defend the place of a reformist trade-union movement in the capitalist system, then you had better be familiar with the statistics on wage rates and the cost of living.

As conceived by Mr. Hansson the school was to contribute in every possible way to the development of the young men and women who came there. It was to provide not alone intellectual stimulus. Workers who had never known the meaning of repose, of leisure, of privacy, were to find them at Brunnsvik. That is why from the beginning a separate room has been provided for each student. This privilege of privacy—"a room of one's own"—should be the experience of each student. They are small rooms, simply furnished, but each has a window looking out through birches to the lake.

Men and women are on a basis of complete equality; education is on exactly the same terms for both sexes. There is, however, a preponderance of men over women as there is in the trade unions. Older men who are married sometimes have their wives come to visit them for a part of the summer. Often among the younger students, and they are in the majority, friendships develop into more serious relationships. A number of marriages have come out of the trade-union school. And the visitor can readily understand this. They stroll along the shady paths or they swim far out beyond the diving pier. At five-thirty they crowd into the dining hall for supper and there is a clamor of young voices. It quiets down and someone at the head table starts a song, "John Brown's Body," it may be, or an old Swedish folk song, or the "Marseillaise." The food is plain, two dishes for the main course, and a simple dessert.

There is little or no external discipline. Rather, a kind of self-discipline is the ideal. This is expressed in a single rule of conduct: *Allting är tillåtet utom det som är dumt eller fult.* Translated freely, this is: You are allowed to do anything you want to do except those things that might be considered stupid or silly. The unions take a pride, naturally, in sending their best men and women. No one has ever had to be expelled from the school. That would be a disgrace not only to the individual but to the union that sent him.

Altogether there are 374 hours of formal instruction during the three months' term. One of the most important courses is devoted to trade-union theory and practice. Mr. Hansson himself gave this course of 51 hours until his retirement. And his lectures were supplemented in the 1937 term by special talks given by August Lindberg, head of the trade-union federation, Gunnar Andersson, secretary, and other officials. Another important course is political science, taught for most of the term by Alf Johansson, a professor at Stockholm University. There is a special course in unemployment insurance, in the international organization of labor, in the history of the labor movement, in statistics. Gunnar Hirdman, head of the Workers' Educational Association, gives a course of 30 hours on "Socialism and the Labor Movement Abroad."

The school pays good salaries and can obtain therefore some of the most able economists and sociologists in the country. Leaders in their respective fields are pleased to come to Brunnsvik for varying periods. It goes without saying that only those professors who have a definite and sympathetic interest in the labor movement and labor politics are chosen. Gösta Bagge, Professor of Economics at Stockholm University and head of the conservative party, would scarcely be invited, for example. Besides teachers who are already recognized authorities, the school has followed the wise policy of bringing in brilliant younger men such as Torsten Gårdlund, candidate for the Doctor of Philosophy degree in economics at Stockholm. In the summer of 1937 Mr. Gårdlund gave a 36-hour course in sociology and social psychology.

Then too, from time to time through the summer special lecturers visit the school. As I have said, Gustaf Söderlund, head of the Employers' Association, pays an annual visit and submits at the conclusion of his talk to an extended cross-examination. Speakers representing a wide range of political and economic beliefs are welcomed. In the summer of 1937 one of the lecturers was Ture Nerman, a Communist member of the Parliament, who gave an account of his visit to Loyalist Spain.

The cost of the course, thirteen weeks including food and lodging, is 225 kronor. This is paid by the union sending the students. Most of those who come to Brunnsvik are employed. They must obtain a leave of absence for the three months but provision for this is made in all wage contracts signed by the trade unions. Sometimes an employer balks at granting leave. Ordinarily in such instances it is only necessary to call this to the attention of the Employers' Association. Now and then, according to the students themselves, employers have been known to find an excuse for laying off workers upon their return from Brunnsvik.

Besides the three months' course there are shorter courses for groups from various trade unions within the federation. The Carpenters' Union sends fifty men for two weeks of study. The following fortnight the Metal Workers come for their course, next the Textile Workers, then the Typographers, and so on. During the 1936 term 635 men and women representing twelve different unions came to Brunnsvik to take these specialized courses. Usually the course includes the study of special problems in organizing the workers in the particular field covered by the union; the conduct of meetings and rules of order; the union's system of unemployment insurance. It includes, too, a quick survey of the history and economics of the industry itself.

While the school is closed during the winter, it is put to a special use during Christmas week. At that time professors of economics and political science from Sweden, Norway, Finland, and Denmark, all of them concerned with labor politics and labor policy, gather for a conference. Some of them are undersecretaries, supervising unemployment insurance, or some other phase of the work of the Ministry of Social Affairs. There are always a number of younger men who may some day play an active part in the labor movement. And there are leaders in the Swedish trade-union federation.

It is the federation that pays for this party. That is just what it is—a kind of house party. During the five days from December 27 to December 31 there is very little sleeping done by anyone. A continuous discussion goes on, interspersed with a great deal of gaiety. It is a rare form of international exchange, with ideas passing back and forth as though international boundaries did not exist. At these conferences there are as many as 75 or 80 delegates, men and women from the four countries.

The Swedish federation, being a hard-boiled organization, does not put on these Christmas house parties merely as a contribution to the gaiety of nations. The underlying motive is to secure the ideas, the advice, the counsel, the good will of the intellectuals. The Christmas week conference is regarded as worthwhile if only because it helps to maintain a working relationship between intellectuals and the trade unions. There is a keen awareness that in other countries, conspicuously in Great Britain, this relationship has been disrupted, to the great loss of both parties.

In many ways the scope of the labor school at Brunnsvik has been broadened. Visiting students come not only from the other Scandinavian countries but from England and the United States. The capacity of the school is taxed and yet each year the list of applicants grows and pressure from the unions desiring to send more of their promising young men and women increases. And this is not surprising since the usefulness of the school is demonstrated again and again. At least ten graduates have advanced to important paid positions in the trade-union field. Others direct study circles, work at organization, and in many ways take an aggressive part in the labor movement. Torvald Karlbom, a graduate of the course in 1929, has succeeded Mr. Hansson as director of the school.

But while it is obvious that it would be possible to make use of greatly enlarged facilities, there is a realization that perhaps this would be unwise. In the size of the school is one of its advantages. And it seems to me that the recognition of this fact is a clew to the common sense of those who have created the institution. Enlarged, something of the atmosphere that prevails today would be lost. There is under discussion the possibility of a second school, similar to that at Brunnsvik.

Dr. Hansson—to give him his academic title—does not conceal his pride in the institution to which he has contributed so much. "I have worked too hard," he says. "Now that I have gone to the Ministry of Social Affairs, they have obtained three men to do my work." But in more serious vein he adds that the time had come for him to retire. His point of view was changing, perhaps becoming more conservative. Each year he was growing one year older than the pupils. In addition to his work as director of the school he formerly edited the federation journal and did one or two other jobs on the side. Now he has become head of the division of the Ministry of Social Affairs dealing with unemployment insurance. Of course, his interest in the trade-union movement continues. He attended the Christmas week conference at Brunnsvik in 1937 and delivered a lecture that served to stir heated discussion. While he has stepped aside, he remains in the role of an anxious grandparent who keeps a close watch on the career of the second generation.

The other institution at Brunnsvik, the People's College, is just as typical in its way of the forces that have created the trade-union movement and the Labor party. And that is true of Norway and Denmark as well as of Sweden, although in Sweden the link between the folk school and the labor movement is much closer. The Brunnsvik People's College was started in 1906 by Karl-Erik Forsslund and a group of associates who were interested in fostering the study of the background and customs of Dalarna and particularly of the region around Brunnsvik. It was a kind of carry-over from the idealism of an earlier day. The study of nature was to have an important part in the curriculum. The emphasis was to be placed on the human spirit and its ennoblement through closer harmony with all forms of culture. These same motives, so typical of the period, were responsible for the folk high schools that came into existence throughout all of Scandinavia at this time.

That was the objective of Forsslund, who seems to have had

the almost mystical love of nature which is sometimes a part of the Swedish temperament. Very soon after its start the direction of the school was changed. Almost from the first support came from labor groups, and increasingly the school was brought within the sphere of trade-union educational activity. Rickard Sandler, Foreign Minister in the present government, was one of the first teachers at the People's College, going there shortly after he received his university degree in 1907. This was in the family tradition as his father was head of the People's College at Hola. But the younger Sandler was acutely aware of the need to broaden the influence of the folk schools by drawing in the mass of organized workers in the trade unions.

The young teacher's wife, Maja Sandler, sharing his views, also took an active part in the workers' educational movement. These two typify this phase of the trade-union movement in Scandinavia. Serious, earnest, giving unstintingly of their energy and their knowledge, they and many others like them constantly stressed the importance of cultural values, of learning for learning's sake, the whole based on a conviction that it is only in this way that there can be lasting social progress. It was Mr. Sandler who in 1912 founded the Workers' Educational Association, designed to send out lecturers, assist in the founding of trade-union libraries, and foster the growth of trade-union study circles.

Both Mr. and Mrs. Sandler worked ardently to promote the Association. In the vigor with which they set out to spread the gospel of education there was not a little of the crusading spirit. Mrs. Sandler tells a story of an early experience as a lecturer that illustrates this zeal. She went into a community in which the interest in these matters was almost nonexistent. Although her lecture had been advertised several days in advance, she found when she reached the hall that there was only a handful of listeners and most of these were old people. Not at all dampened, she asked the president of the study circle where all the young men and women were. He replied somewhat embarrassedly that they were all at another hall dancing and playing cards. "Well, we will go there then," said Mrs. Sandler, and taking her slim audience with her she invaded the other hall. For a time she was unable to make herself heard but finally when there was quiet gave a talk that was a challenge to the young people of the community to start a discussion club. Although at first they listened in resentful silence, the speaker was able finally to start a spirited argument. And out of this argument a discussion group was formed which is still in existence.

The germ of Mr. Sandler's idea for the Workers' Educational Association has grown to remarkable proportions. Today there are nearly 6,000 study circles in Sweden with a membership well over 75,000. While the circles are open to those outside the trade-union movement, by far the majority of persons enrolled for courses are workers. The small minority who do not belong to any workers' organization must pay a higher enrollment fee. The circles are necessarily open to all because the association receives support from public funds. Here is the statement of Gunnar Hirdman, the director, on aims and objectives:

Like the British Workers' Educational Association, the Swedish Association is nonvocational, nonsectarian and nonpolitical. This does not mean that religious and political questions are not studied. On the contrary political science and current events form a very important part of the studies. It does not mean that party programs are not studied; they are taken up in detail but always with an attempt at impartiality. Teachers and lecturers are requested to give a fair interpretation of the problems involved and to let the students know what are facts and what are personal opinions.

The reasons for this policy are threefold. First, financial support is received from the state, the county councils, and the municipalities. An activity financed to some extent from such sources must be nonpolitical. Second, the Workers' Educational Association is the concern of the whole labor movement and its teaching should therefore not favor one section or another. Third, the association stands for free teaching, free research, and free discussion because we believe this method to be the most effective.

Besides public funds, the association is supported by fees paid by affiliated organizations in proportion to membership. These organizations include the Federation of Labor, the Coöperative Union, the Social-Democratic party, the League of Social-Democratic Youth, the federation of Syndicalist unions, and ten lesser labor organizations. In addition there are the fees paid by members taking the study circle courses.

While the instructors and tutors are for the most part self-educated workers, many teachers, and particularly from the folk high schools, participate in this work. Then there are special lecturers sent out by the central office, usually for a series of talks to be given over Saturday and Sunday. Such lecturers can be obtained by the local study circle for 50 kronor for a series of four lectures or 60 kronor for six. Here is a table prepared by Mr. Hirdman for the year 1935–36, showing the popularity of the various subjects offered:

Subjects	Number of Circles	Percentage
Political science, local government, and parliamentary procedure	1,566	25.4
English language	518	8.8
Bookkeeping	393	6.7
Esperanto	348	5.9
Amateur theater	341	5.9
Music	324	5.5
Swedish language, grammar, and essay writing .	295	5.1
Arithmetic	290	4.9
Trade unionism	235	4
Literature	179	3
Socialism	125	2.1

The remaining 22.6 per cent is divided among a range of subjects that rivals the curriculum of a large American university. Labor history, hygiene, economics, German, Finnish, philosophy, psychology, general history, Communism and Leninism, Russian, French, public speaking, history of art, this suggests the scope of instruction offered. Mr. Hirdman, who is in the tradition of the founders of the People's College, serious, earnest, deeply convinced of the value of education, can reel off statistics showing the growth of the movement in the past twenty-five years. There are nearly 1,500 libraries containing 488,000 volumes and in 1936 there were 124,000 borrowers.

Each summer at the People's College at Brunnsvik there are ten two-week courses for study circle leaders, presented by the Workers' Educational Association. Students enrolling for one of these special summer courses devote four hours a day to study of the subject to be taken up by the circle in his or her community. Courses are offered in economics, the Swedish Constitution, local administration, modern philosophy, social psychology, trade unionism, socialism, literature, and history.

Increasingly Mr. Hirdman has sought to give this summer school at Brunnsvik an international character. And this may be because of the international influence in Mr. Hirdman's own development. A metal worker in Dalarna, he began as study leader in Västerås. Later he went to England, France, and Belgium to study adult education, attending summer school in the United States and traveling widely in Russia. At the Brunnsvik summer school in 1937 there were representatives not only from all the Scandinavian countries but from Great Britain as well. A special seminar on international labor problems was held with five or six countries participating from July 20 to 31. According to present plans, this international conference is to be repeated each year, drawing, it is hoped, a more and more representative gathering.

The real reason for the existence of the People's College is the six months' course that is given from October to May. During the first year there are courses in civics, the history of civilization, the social sciences, the Swedish language, mathematics, and bookkeeping. Students who take the second-year course specialize in social and industrial problems and infrequently there is offered an alternate course in the humanities. The students, the majority of whom are trade-union workers, average twenty-three to twenty-four years of age. Tuition is very low and students are usually aided by their union locals.

The People's College and the labor school of the National Federation are separate institutions, although they share the same campus and to a certain degree the same facilities. The People's College is financed, as are other similar schools throughout the country, by central and local government and the revenue from tuition. It happens that the People's College at Brunnsvik has drawn its students almost entirely from trade-union ranks. In a sense it has become an adjunct of the trade-union movement. For this reason, of course, the labor school was established at Brunnsvik.

It should be understood that this educational movement is still in an expanding phase. The man who started the whole study circle idea in Sweden, Oscar Olsson, is still very active.

Mr. Olsson founded the first study group in connection with the activities of the Good Templar organization. Now as the international head of this order and as a member of the first chamber of the Riksdag he continues to promote the development of study groups. They have taken varied forms. Sometimes they are more or less formal, with a teacher who lectures, the students preparing home work as in a school. Other circles are in reality discussion groups or reading groups, conducted in a friendly, informal fashion.

In Denmark there is no such close relationship between the folk high schools and the labor movement as exists in Sweden. In their origin and in their present direction they are much more nearly concerned with the rural population. And they are more concerned, too, with the humanities and with Denmark's cultural past.

The Danish federation of trade unions and the Social-Democratic party together support two labor colleges, one at Esbjerg, founded twenty-seven years ago, and the other at Roskilde, started only in 1931. The latter was established in a folk high school purchased from a private organization. To finance the work of the two schools all trade-union members and all party members are assessed a few cents a year. During the winter there are courses for unemployed trade-union workers. In the summer special instruction is offered to both union and party members. And in September there is a course three weeks in length for active trade-union officials. Related to the two schools, as in Sweden, is a whole complex of study circles and allied activities.

Both party and union organizations underwrite labor's own educational program in Norway, too. There are evening classes, and week-end courses, study circles, and discussion groups. In the northernmost of the Scandinavian countries, however, the stress is more nearly upon learning through doing. Through mass demonstrations and carefully planned exhibitions the rank and file are made to understand the significance of labor's struggle and the importance of organization. The Labor Education Association goes in for making motion pictures, many of them first-rate documentary films showing in a very human and interesting way various phases of trade-union activity. Labor has its own sports league with a membership of more than 60,-000, putting on field meets and all kinds of athletic contests.

The process of learning through doing is, in the theory of modern education, far more effective than academic instruction. There is perhaps too much of the routine and the stereotyped in the older educational programs. I have heard this view expressed by alert younger Laborites who were also critical, as I have said, of party newspapers and other publications.

Often, the complaint is, party and trade-union leaders follow a policy of petty economy with respect to propaganda. They think still in traditional and outworn terms. It is a frequent complaint that the salaries paid on party newspapers and magazines are so low that inevitably the result is inferior work. This is, as many young Laborites are themselves aware, a dangerously short-sighted policy. If the mass of the people are to listen in an age in which there are an infinite number of distractions, the accent must be clear and unmistakable, in the language of the moment. The halting, uncertain voice that is all too obviously out of the past will never be heard.

CHAPTER VII

SIT DOWN IN THE KITCHEN

IT was what people muttered to each other at the time that the motor strikes were on in Detroit. "But what if it happened in your own kitchen? If your cook decided to go on a sit-down strike? What would you do then?" The very suggestion was meant to strike terror to the heart of the householder. There was invoked a sinister picture of a large determined woman sitting with folded arms on top, presumably, of the gas stove. It was somehow the final indignity, the ultimate crime.

In Denmark, which is one of the most orderly and peaceful countries in the world, it could happen, this dreadful thing. It could happen because cooks and housemaids, or the best cooks and housemaids at any rate, are organized into a trade union. I say it could happen. To my knowledge it never has and I doubt very much that it ever will. In fact Danish housewives scarcely give it a thought. They are too grateful for the benefits that this unique trade union has brought them.

The whole thing began with Marie Christensen. Marie Christensen is to my way of thinking a shining example of what that very much overworked word *service* means. Her example gives meaning to most of the hoary platitudes about doing better than anyone else the kind of job you find yourself in, being a better builder of mousetraps and all the rest of it. Starry-eyed idealists who would remake the world by the magic of a vocabulary might well take a lesson or two from Marie Christensen. She is the kind of idealist who believes in tackling the task that is immediately at hand; which is usually harder, much harder, than joining the crowd forever rushing off to find the frontier of utopia.

At the turn of the century Marie Christensen, a young girl then, was a general servant in a Copenhagen household. The hours were long, as they are all over the world, and the wages were very low. Coming of a working-class household and with some awareness of the significance of the labor movement, this young servant realized that in her trade there were no standards whatsoever. Neither employer nor worker had any pattern of behavior to follow; for both the relationship was largely a gamble.

In November, 1899, young Marie succeeded in organizing the nucleus of the Household Assistants' Trade Union. They were not servants—it was an important distinction—they were household assistants. From the outset one of the main objectives of the union was a training school which should turn out servants —no, household assistants—who would be skilled in the arts of the home. Toward this goal Miss Christensen worked with tireless energy in the hours that she could take off from her job. She talked, she wrote, she interviewed public officials. From every possible source she sought support and contributions for her training school.

The Household Assistants' Trade Union grew slowly. For a variety of reasons it has never achieved a membership of more than a few thousand. But out of it has come the training school that Marie Christensen dreamed about and that in itself is ample tribute first to the power of organization and second, and probably more important in this instance, to the persistence of an individual with an idea.

In remodeled quarters in Copenhagen's Rosengaarden, the school at the start in 1906 was modest enough. But from the first Miss Christensen, as director, insisted on rigorous standards. The girls who were graduated from the school should know all that it was possible to know about cooking and the kitchen, including the elements of dietetics, cleaning and the laundry, and the care of children; to say nothing of such details as proper service at table, simple needlework, the arrangement of furniture in a room and flowers in a vase; plus certain contributions to general knowledge, that is, the theories of conduct behind the practical household arts.

No sooner was the school organized in Rosengaarden than Miss Christensen began to lay plans for a larger building that should really be adapted to the needs of such a school. Once again she waged an unceasing campaign. And through the years she succeeded in enlisting the interest of the central government and the city of Copenhagen. For the Household Assistants' Trade School was proving its worth over and over, producing such exceptional servants that the supply could not possibly meet the demand.

Eventually the state and the city were to contribute fairly substantial sums and this money together with funds accumulated by the trade union made it possible to construct a new building. It was just twenty years after the opening of the original school that Miss Christensen took part in the ceremony dedicating the new structure. Prime Minister Stauning was there and in his speech praised not only the work of the school but its founder. Students in black-and-white maid's uniform stood in a row along the foundation beneath the beams that were decked in traditional green. Taking her place beside the Prime Minister, Miss Christensen put the cornerstone in place. It does not take a great deal of imagination to realize what this day meant in Marie Christensen's life.

The new school is a handsome four-story structure of simple design, done in warm-colored brick with a red tile roof. Facing on the street are a laundry, a delicatessen, and a restaurant, all run by students at the school. Metal letters across one façade spell out "Household Assistants' Trade School." Besides being a school it is, in a sense, a laboratory of the household arts where new methods and new devices are tested by experts in their respective fields.

At the start the trade school was open only to members of the union. But since contributions have come from state and city, enrollment is open to anyone. The state makes an annual contribution of about $3,000, the city about $800 and other communities throughout Denmark smaller sums. Tuition and profits from the laundry and the delicatessen and restaurant make up most of the budget which is sufficient to provide training courses, both short and long, for about five hundred girls each year.

The beginners' course, for girls from sixteen to twenty years old, is of six months' duration, divided as follows: ten weeks in the kitchen, five weeks in the bakery, five weeks in the laundry, and five weeks for cleaning, serving, and sewing. The girls live at the school, which has accommodations for about one hundred

bove: Ceremony at dedication of Household Assistants' Trade School; Prime Minister Stauning standing, Marie Christensen seated.

elow: One of the kitchens in the Household Assistants' Trade School.

and twenty in rooms furnished with a Spartan simplicity and kept immaculate with the zeal for cleanliness and order that amounts in Denmark to a kind of mania. The time of these beginners is very carefully scheduled so that they will get the most out of the course. Besides practical instruction in the basic tasks they hear lectures on the budgeting of household accounts, on interior decoration, on dietetic standards, and so forth. For all this the tuition is ten dollars a month and there are a number of scholarships for those who do not have that sum.

In the second half of the year virtually the same beginners' course is given to young women who are about to marry. The objective is to create efficient housekeepers for young men of modest income. This phase of the school is the result of the subsidy from the state. Spending less time in the kitchen, the bakery, and the laundry, the young brides-to-be have three hundred hours during their six months allotted to the school nursery. Here are from six to ten babies ranging in age from a few weeks up to two years. For the most part the children of unmarried mothers, they are cared for until adoption by students who work under the supervision of instructors. The fee again is ten dollars a month and there are scholarships or partial scholarships for girls who cannot pay.

Besides these basic courses for beginning housemaids and beginning housewives, the school offers specialized instruction. Prospective nursemaids must spend eight hundred and fifty hours during a six months' course in the nursery. There are evening courses in table decoration and serving, in the preparation of jams and preserves, in laundering. For those who have completed the beginners' course, three months of specialized instruction is offered leading to a position as chef or assistant director of a restaurant, and in another department the advanced student can in three months acquire the skills necessary to be a housekeeper, the head of a large establishment. Each year about two hundred and fifty women take these special courses.

There is always a long waiting list at the school and it is not surprising, since completion of the training means an immediate advance in status and salary. (The prospective bride is ready to be married with the confidence that she can run her future husband's house to the best possible advantage.) Young girls who take the beginning course have their wages doubled and they can be assured that, granted a normal degree of constancy, they need never be without a job. Those who take advanced courses, particularly older women with experience, can earn, when allowance is made for the value of room, board, and uniforms, considerably more than factory or even office workers. If the waiting list for entrance to the Household Assistants' School is long, the list of applicants who want to employ graduates is much longer. In Denmark, as everywhere else in the world, a well-trained household assistant is a much sought after prize.

Even the casual visitor is made aware of how much Marie Christensen has contributed to the success of the school, to the spirit of good will that seems to pervade the entire institution. She is simple, friendly, but you feel at once that she will accomplish what she sets out to accomplish. It is in the firm line of her mouth and the determined set of her chin. In her efficient looking office she explains the purpose of the school and why it was started. However, you do not doubt for a moment that she could go into the kitchen and produce an almond cake or an apple tart of unquestioned superiority.

It is her pleasure to show visitors through the school. The girls' sleeping rooms and even their living and study quarters are so precisely ordered that an American is inevitably reminded of West Point; the bedside table in the same exact spot, vase of flowers in the middle, the spread tucked under the pillow, slippers on the small rug. On the walls of the big study, as in any other girls' school, are rows of photographs of successive graduating classes, fresh-faced, apple-cheeked, cook's or nurse's caps over straw-colored hair.

The bakery, at this particular hour of the day at any rate, is the most attractive spot in the building. A large, light room, it is filled with the spicy smell that comes from crisp, delicate pastry just out of the oven. It is the pastry which is the specialty of the country and the class has just completed a laboratory experiment in which, if the test of sight and smell prevail, each of the twenty-five students must have achieved perfection. Miss Christensen picks out a sample to present to the visitor, looking about at her girls with a quick, friendly smile.

The nursery has a hospital whiteness and cleanliness. Here,

too, the director appears to be perfectly at home even though she is a spinster. To a student who is preparing the feeding for the smaller children she gives a word of advice. The windows of the nursery look out onto a sunny courtyard where the older youngsters have been turned out to play on the grass. While there is every evidence of the efficiency with which this department of the school is conducted, it somehow escapes the blight of institutionalism. You feel that these children receive their just share of affection.

In the laundry there is every kind of labor-saving device from stationary tubs of white enamel to the latest type of mangle. Nearby are linen closets which are a demonstration, too, of household efficiency and order. In the restaurant that is run by the school Miss Christensen insists upon the visitor having a meal. She is proud of the service and proud of the satisfied customers who come back year after year to the school restaurant. The prices are modest, in keeping with the neighborhood, but the food is excellent and the choice not too limited. At the door Marie Christensen says good-bye to her visitor and there is the curious sense that it is not only a school but a home; for all the two hundred and fifty students and twenty or thirty teachers, a home that Marie Christensen has created.

Despite the success of the school, the Household Assistants' Trade Union has not enrolled more than three or four thousand members at any one time. The reason, according to those who are familiar with the history of the union, is the large turnover that takes place in this field. Particularly in recent decades girls tend to look upon household service as something temporary. They want to marry or, failing that, they are looking for high cash wages in a factory or an office. In a "regular job" they have had the assurance that hours of work would be definitely restricted and that when quitting time came, they would leave work behind them.

It was this very problem that Miss Christensen sought to solve through the union. And the standards that have come to be accepted in urban areas are largely the result of the activity of the union. For though the organization has never achieved any overwhelming numerical strength, it has had a wide influence, if only through the example of the excellence of union housemaids. Hours off and scheduled holidays are much more scrupulously respected by Copenhagen housewives than in the days when there was no organization at all.

What it lacks in size, the union makes up in solidarity. A full-time president is employed who devotes her energies to organization and improvement of standards. Succeeding Miss Christensen in this office was Wilhelmina Johnson. The head of the Copenhagen branch is Erna Olsen who despite her marriage gives a great deal of time and devotion to the work. This is true of the more enthusiastic members whose interest continues after their marriage.

One of the most conspicuous achievements of the union is a home for elderly housemaids built in 1935. The total cost was nearly $200,000. Again the aid of the state was enlisted when approximately $15,000 had been raised by the organization. Primarily it is an apartment house where "household assistants" too old to work can obtain small but comfortable flats for only a nominal rent. Service goes with these flats at the option of the tenant. But also there are twenty apartments free for those who cannot pay. The building is in the modern style with many windows. It is a beginning, one must remember, just as the school is a beginning, and the union, too.

Plans are now under preparation for the establishment of a similar school at Aarhus in the province of Jutland. The town has offered to give the ground and $12,500 as an initial construction subsidy. The Copenhagen school has been so singularly successful that it was the model for one just like it started by the Polish government at Warsaw. And in Sweden, too, they have taken it for a model, a similar school having been started at Stockholm. The reputation of this remarkable institution and the girls who are graduated from it has in fact spread to all of Europe. In London if you can manage to get a trained Danish servant on the labor quota it is the occasion for wild rejoicing.

For the outsider it is difficult to assign the credit for this unique achievement. There is nothing false in Marie Christensen's modest insistence that it could not have happened without the union. That is quite obvious. But it is obvious too that the union would never have happened without Marie Christensen.

CHAPTER VIII

"COMPANY TOWN"

IT is a phrase with distinctly unpleasant connotations—"company town." A huddle of bleak, gray houses about a mine shaft or a factory is the picture that is ordinarily evoked. Or it may be a model community, carefully designed by the company's architect; with "outside agitators," that is, trade-union organizers, excluded from this little paradise. Prior to the abolition of the coal and iron police in Pennsylvania, company towns in that state combined the worst features of both types. Company police patrolled what were virtually walled towns—a squalid collection of miserable dwellings, barring all aliens.

In Scandinavia "company town" means something quite different. In fact it is a kind of slander to apply this term at all. In the north of Europe it is possible to find towns in which there is but a single industry, virtually all the houses company owned, and yet these towns are completely unionized and, moreover, they are governed in certain instances from the Left, by Socialists and Communists. So far as I could find there was no suggestion on either side that a man might be coerced or intimidated because he rented his house from the company for which he worked. The relationship between employee and employer appeared to be on the same independent footing as in any larger community. While such independence was taken for granted by everyone, it seemed to the visitor more or less familiar with America's company towns an extraordinary phenomenon.

The towns that have been built around Sweden's new mineral industry in the north illustrate very well the care that is taken, first, to provide a decent environment for several thousand families and, second, to preserve the independence of the relationship between employer and employee. And perhaps equally important is the constant care that is exercised to preserve the natural balance; to upset as little as possible the ancient harmony of air, earth, and water. This last is the note that is steadily emphasized by company officials. One facet of the love of nature which so strongly marks the national character is a deep resentment of the uglier aspects of industrialism, the darkened skies and befouled air, all the blank, awful hideousness of large-scale industry. Human beings should not be subjected to such indignities is the feeling.

The principal gold mine in this new development is at Boliden, about 350 miles north and somewhat east of Stockholm. About two hours distant from Boliden by motor is Skellefteåhamn, on the shores of the Baltic, where the great smeltery is located. Recently still another mine has been developed at Laver, north of Boliden, in rough, heavily forested country where even in summer stray remnants of Lapp reindeer herds may occasionally be seen. All three are owned and operated by one company under the direction of Mr. Oscar Falkman, a quiet-spoken engineer, who is chiefly responsible for the high standards achieved in this remote outpost of industry.

The smeltery employs the largest number of workers. At Skellefteåhamn there are about 1,100 members of the local branch of the Metal Workers' Union. This includes all the employees in the plant, electricians and carpenters as well as those who are actually engaged in the smelting and refining of the ore that comes from Boliden. The average rate of pay is 350 kronor, or somewhat less than $100, for about 200 hours a month. The wage contract between the company and the union calls for an eight-hour day and a six-day week. This contract, in accord with the constitution of the federation of trade unions, provides that the Metal Workers shall have the exclusive bargaining right for all employees in the plant.

A week's holiday at full pay is provided under the contract but the new law now insures a two weeks' holiday. Workers who must fill shifts on legal holidays—the plant is in continuous operation—are given extra time off in accord with another provision of the contract. It provides also for free medical care by the company's physicians for all employees and care for their families at a very low rate.

In this matter of health, it may be said here, the company takes extraordinary precautions. There are frequent examinations by fluoroscope and X-ray to determine whether any symptoms of lung trouble are present. There have been several changes in plant techniques to reduce the dust content of the air and thereby prevent silicosis. In the building in which the blast furnaces are a powerful ventilating system changes the air every minute and a half. Similarly a close check is kept on nasal passages where dust may do damage. At the least sign of any illness a man is sent home on sick pay as provided for in the union contract. Sick pay is almost the equivalent of the full wage rate.

Tiled showers and locker rooms, where each man changes into work clothes and bathes at the end of his shift, are provided. The company also furnished the space and the equipment for a dining room. But it is run on a coöperative basis by the men themselves, with no aid or interference from the company. Functional in the best sense, with large windows and a complete absence of decoration as such, the huge dining room achieves a kind of distinction.

Arsenic is one of the minerals contained in the ore from Boliden and Laver. In fact there is more arsenic produced at Skellefteåhamn than anywhere else in the world, the volume of production every three days being sufficient to poison the entire population of the world. An enormous warehouse holds 200,000 tons of refined arsenic and Swedish technicians are busy promoting new uses for the stuff. Exceptional precautions are taken to protect the health of those who work with this mineral. At the end of each work period the men are required to bathe and change clothes.

The community itself is about one mile from the plant, with a street-car service to take the men to and from work. Laid out by company architects, the town is built around two institutions —the church and the Folketshus. This People's House was built by the union with the help of a substantial contribution from the company. It is the center of all trade-union activity. Here are the union offices, furnished with taste and an eye to efficiency. And in the Folketshus is an auditorium with a seating capacity of 400. Movies are shown in this hall, the union having entire charge and fixing the price of admission. It is the scene of important union gatherings and special celebrations of various kinds, in short, the focus of the life of the town. There are other smaller meeting rooms and kitchen facilities so that meals may be served on special occasions. Similarly the company contributed to the construction of the church, done in the modern style.

The institution of the Folketshus has played a very interesting part in the rise of the Swedish labor movement. In the early days a tactical measure often was to build a Folketshus as soon as possible in an unorganized community. It was not only a stronghold, a place where meetings could be held without interference, but it was also the center of entertainment and enlightenment, a weapon against the dullness and boredom of the countryside.

The Folketsparks that began to develop early in the 'nineties served a similar function. Now almost every community has such a park, with a café, a dancing floor, and a People's Theater. Most of the buildings were built by the workers themselves during the long summer evenings and on Sundays. They are cultural centers in the truest sense of the phrase.

A friend in Sweden writes about a visit to Kolbeck, in Västmanland, an industrial community of about 3,700 inhabitants with many farm and agricultural workers round about. The nearest town of any size is more than fifty miles away and the Folketspark has become the center of life for the whole region. It takes little imagination to realize what such an institution meant when there was no other place except the public road where meetings could be held.

In the office of the secretary at the Folketshus at Skellefteåhamn the records of this solidly organized union are kept. The union receives in dues about 6,000 kronor a month, of which about 4,000 kronor are sent to the district office and the balance retained to defray local costs. Incidentally, the collection of dues in the trade-union movement in Scandinavia is not a major problem; delinquencies have in recent years been negligible. Unemployment benefits are paid from the district office, but in this instance the plant local is for all practical purposes the district since otherwise it includes only small machine shops.

At the time of my visit there were only about 130 members of the union unemployed. They were eligible for unemployment benefits from their union, the minimum being one kronor a

Above: General view of plant and docks of the Boliden Corporation at Skellefteåhamn.

Below: Houses built for employees at Skellefteåhamn by Boliden Corporation.

day, going up to approximately twenty-one kronor a week for members of long standing.

To aid in the formation of this union in a new industry men long experienced in trade-union organization and activity came up from the south of Sweden. They were also skilled metal workers and so they were assured of a job immediately. The first paid secretary of the local, Adamson, came from the south. He resigned to take a place in the offices of the federation at Stockholm and was replaced by Carlström who also came from the south and participated in the formation of the Skellefteå-hamn local. This paid executive holds his job from year to year while the other officers are elected annually.

At the time that the big plant was constructed housing was, of course, a major problem. The company built a comparatively small number of dwelling units, for technicians and young engineers as well as for general workers. These are for the most part two and four family houses, done in stained wood with red tile roofs, well adapted to the wooded setting in which they are situated. Most units consist of a good sized kitchen-dining room, a living room, and bedroom or sleeping alcove. They have electric cooking stoves and toilets but no central heating. The rent is approximately one seventh of income.

It would have been fairly simple for the company to have continued to build houses as the pay roll increased. But Mr. Falkman was of the opinion that it was much better for men to own their homes. The relationship might tend toward paternalism, he feared, if the company provided all housing. Therefore workers have been encouraged to build with loans at low interest rates or to buy or rent in the near-by town of Skellefteå. The company houses serve, however, as a kind of yardstick on standards and costs.

In various ways the employees in the plant are encouraged to raise gardens. For the gardens judged best each year the company provides prizes. Partly this comes out of Mr. Falkman's desire to preserve the natural balance. Most of the workers have been drawn from the surrounding country. Formerly they lived by farming. It would be unwise to divorce them too completely from an ancient way of life, Mr. Falkman reasons, for the time will come when the ore is exhausted. Or some shift in world trade or the technics of industry might seriously affect the plant. Then these families would find it very difficult to return to the old method of getting a living. We do not want to separate them entirely from nature, Mr. Falkman says.

The company employs an expert whose chief duty it is to observe the effect of waste gases on the vegetation of the surrounding countryside. And this, it must be remembered, is in remote northern country, covered largely by scrub pine and birch. So that no injury would be done to surrounding stands of timber the company built a plant to extract sulphur from sulphur dioxide, one of the principal waste gases discharged from the huge smokestack. Believed to be the only one of its kind in the world, it was built despite the fact that the world sulphur market has been pretty well ruined by dumping on the part of Italy and Russia.

Some pine trees within a short radius of the plant have possibly been affected by the small volume of sulphur dioxide which is not treated. Deciduous trees have been planted which will replace the pines if they have actually been destroyed. In addition the company has paid small amounts to a few farmers although their claims, in the opinion of the company's expert, were very dubious. Similarly claims were brought against the company by farmers and fishermen for defiling a stream near the mine at Boliden. These claims were paid and the company then took elaborate precautions to insure that no impurities would reach the stream in the future.

In planning the mining operation at Boliden great care was taken, as at Skellefteåhamn, to upset the natural balance as little as possible. The entire community—houses, coöperative store, Folketshus, church, hotel—was built by the company. It is an example of skilful planning, the town being so laid out that the mining operation intrudes as little as possible on the private lives of workers and technicians. The stripping is carefully disposed of. Excavations within the mine are being filled up when work along a vein is completed.

The rate of pay for miners is 2 kronor, 30 öre—about 60 cents—an hour. Ordinarily there are two shifts in the mine, each shift divided into two four-hour periods. After working four hours the men come up for lunch and a rest of an hour. Then they go back and work the second half of the shift.

Laver, hidden away in the endless pine forests, is the newest development. Every effort was made, in constructing this community, to profit from earlier experience. For example, a heating plant was built by the company to provide heat for all houses and offices at Laver. This, it was estimated, would be far more economical, particularly in view of the problem involved in obtaining coal over mountain roads from the nearest railway junction. Two and three family units are the rule at Laver, the dwellings being rather more spacious than at either Boliden or Skellefteåhamn. Rents average 40 kronor a month which includes heat from the central plant and running water.

Wage negotiations for the new local formed at Laver were carried on with the company by Edvard Mattson, national head of the Miners' Union. At the outset Edvard Mattson bargained over conditions of living when the development was still in process of construction. For example, he sought to obtain from the company as large a contribution as possible for the Folketshus. And it was agreed at the start that the union should operate in the Folketshus the only restaurant at Laver, the company merely specifying that it should come up to certain standards.

In the first contract the wage scale at Laver was not so high as at Boliden and union leaders were willing to accept the fact of a differential. They reasoned in this way. Virtually all of the new workers were drawn from the surrounding countryside. The wage provided in the contract seemed to them phenomenally large, more than they had ever received before. But as they take an increasing part in the activity of the union, they become more and more aware of the significance of the differential and it will not be many years before they will obtain by their own efforts the higher scale. In this way the rank and file will be far more impressed with the importance of solidarity than if the highest wage scale had been obtained without effort.

The controlling shares in the Boliden corporation were originally held by Ivar Kreuger. At the time of his suicide they were pledged to the Skandinaviska Bank. Some apprehension existed lest they should fall into the hands of foreigners and an immediate outcry arose at the possibility that this important national

resource might pass out of Swedish control. The bank reëstab-
lished the right to the shares but meanwhile such a controversy
had arisen that the directors of the company decided everything
possible should be done to reassure the public. For this reason
the sum of 750,000 kronor was set aside to be used for the re-
settlement of employees when, and if, the store of minerals is
exhausted. The money, it is now contemplated, will be put to a
variety of purposes, such as transferring workers to other centers where employment exists and compensating those who have
built their own homes. The fund is to be expended under the
joint direction of the company and the state.

The men responsible for the Boliden company are not altru-
ists or social planners as such. They are keenly aware of the importance of having the good will not only of labor but of the
general public. A company that is privileged to exploit a natural resource must be on its good behavior; it must respond to
the pressure of public opinion. To act otherwise would be to
jeopardize what is the very life of the company. This is said
without seeking to detract in any way from the credit which is
due to Mr. Falkman for the intelligence that he has brought to
his task.

In dealing with the union Mr. Falkman drives a shrewd bargain, using every possible advantage. The company makes sure
that the men realize all that a strike would mean. If work were
suspended, the furnaces would have to be entirely reconstructed
and the large stack, which has not been allowed to cool since its
construction three years ago, would have to undergo major re-
pairs. This would mean a shut-down of two months, and so if a
strike were to last for a month, the men would be out of work a
total of at least three months.

Ever since its start the company has been extremely prosperous. Perhaps we could pay a higher wage scale than other firms
in the same field, the directors say, but we would not want to if
it would mean that other companies would have to meet such a
scale. The Boliden firm is, of course, affiliated with the Swedish
Employers' Association and is bound by its rules and regulations.

The directors of the company have a political bias which is a
factor in employment. The Miners' Union is regarded as among
the more radical organizations within the Trade-Union Federa-

tion, particularly in the north. About 10 to 15 per cent of the employees of the Boliden company are Communists although it is said that they play little part in the leadership of the union. When for some reason or other the force must be reduced, these workers are likely to be discharged first. But if they are employees of long standing or if they have families dependent upon them, then the union will not allow them to be discharged; that would be too obvious discrimination. We make no effort to spy out Communists, the directors say, but the foremen soon learn who they are even though they make no public profession of their political beliefs.

But the important fact is that collective bargaining is as much accepted business practice of this company as modern cost accounting. The fact that there is no other source of industrial employment within a radius of a hundred miles or more does not alter the process in the least. It is a part of accepted civilized behavior. We have never had a strike or any serious differences with labor, Mr. Falkman says with distinct pride. And the same thing is expressed in a different way by Mr. Mattson, for the union, when he says, "We get along with the company very well."

It is interesting to note that the company buys all of its power from the town of Skellefteå, which operates a series of hydroelectric plants on the Skellefteå River. The company's annual power bill is about a half million kronor a year, at the rate of about 1¼ öre a kilowatt hour. Domestic rates in the town today are about 15 öre a kilowatt hour. And the town of Skellefteå enjoys an exceptionally low tax rate thanks to the operation of the power plant which is selling its capacity production. Of this relationship, too, the directors speak with a certain pride, for they are aware of what it means in the good will not only of the immediate community but the nation at large.

Another company that is aware of the importance of public good will is the Luossavaara-Kirunavaara Aktiebolaget, shortened to L.K.A.B., which operates the great iron mines in Lapland at Kiruna well within the Arctic Circle. The town of Kiruna is governed by a council which is made up of fourteen Communists, thirteen Social-Democrats, four Conservatives, four National Socialists, one Folk party member, and one Swedish Communist. It is here in the far north, as the composition of the town council indicates, that political extremes are to be found. Most of the members of the council, including virtually all the Socialists and Communists, are employed by the company.

Until recently the two majority parties were in opposition to each other most of the time, engaging in factional quarrels with the result that the conservative minority swung the balance. Of late they have come to an agreement that is in part the result of their mutual interest in the Spanish civil war. Altogether the town of Kiruna has sent out more than 30,000 kronor for the Spanish government forces. On at least two occasions union members have contributed a day's pay, amounting to 8,000 kronor, adding this to a fund voted from the union treasury.

It is this radical town council that fixes the tax rates paid by the company and the 1,800 employees and their families who make up the population of the Kommun. The income tax rate is a flat 7.75 per cent applied on all income above 1,000 kronor a year. Besides the tax on income the same rate is applied to 5 per cent of the value of all personal property. This rate represents a reduction from 9.80 per cent. It is now the same as that applied by the city of Stockholm. And in addition the Kommun receives a considerable sum from the royalty which L.K.A.B. pays to the Swedish state for the right to exploit the iron ore that is a source of such great wealth.

A wide variety of social services is maintained by the Kommun, subsidized in part by the company. The school system at Kiruna is one of the finest in Sweden, including an excellent school for training young people in special skills. This training school for boys and girls who have finished the regular course was started by Hjalmar Lindbohm, for many years managing director of the company, as a means of relieving the problem of unemployment in the community. Comparatively few youths were absorbed in the mines and the problem was to train them so that they could be placed in jobs to the south where there was a larger labor market. Last year there were about one hundred and twenty boys and sixty girls in this school, ranging from fourteen to nineteen years of age. The boys are instructed in a variety of skills in demand in modern industry and the

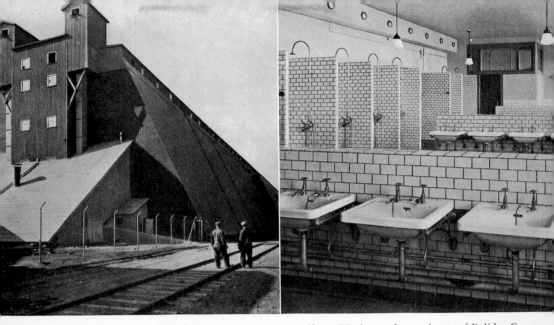

Above: Arsenic warehouse at Skellefteåhamn.

Above: Washroom for employees of Boliden Corporation at smeltery at Skellefteåhamn.

Below: Lumber workers in the north for whom a minimum wage law has been adopted.

training is of such a high standard that there is a constant demand in industrial cities to the south for boys who have completed the four-year course. The girls are taught along the general line of the Swedish housekeeping school, with courses in cooking, laundry, sewing, weaving, and child care, and for the most part they remain in Kiruna. As part of the course in child care, children under two years of age may be left at the school from 8 A.M. to 5 P.M. and they are cared for by the girls in the class, who are under expert supervision, for five cents a day.

The company has continued to provide 40 per cent of the cost of maintaining this craft school, 20 per cent of the balance coming from the state, and the remainder from revenue received by the school for its services and products. This was all very well as an aid in relieving the small volume of unemployment that occurred prior to 1929. But with the world slump the jobless were a serious problem in Kiruna. The community, as the operations in the mines were cut to lower and lower levels, became an "island of unemployment."

To meet this situation the council voted to establish a training school and farm at Stjärnsund in Dalecarlia, a day's journey to the south. At this colony in central Sweden the town supports sixty young men from fifteen to twenty-five years of age. There is no fixed curriculum at Stjärnsund. New arrivals help with the work on the farm or in the workshops and receive some formal education in the school until jobs are found for them. Stjärnsund is maintained by the town of Kiruna and the state, and by the sale of products from the farm and workshop, including hospital beds and stainless steel kitchenware. Since the armament boom, and the unprecedented demand for Swedish iron ore, the problem of unemployment in Kiruna has not been acute. Nevertheless the local training school and the farm colony at Stjärnsund have been maintained.

In recent years the Kiruna miners have become more conservative. The decline of Communist influence dates from a sympathetic strike that was called in 1928 at the instigation of younger and more radical members of the Miners' Union. At that time there was a strike of miners in the south and while wages were high in Kiruna, the younger element carried the day and the sympathy strike was called. This strike lasted for eight months and ended in a stalemate. At the same time the Communist leadership advised a strike against taxes with the result that back assessments accumulated. The effects of the worldwide depression began to be felt in 1930 and many miners in 1937 were still paying back taxes and back rents.

Similarly the Syndicalist union has declined in recent years. In 1933 it had a membership of 850 which was close to that of the regular union. This has dwindled to less than 400 members. During the past four years no one has left the regular union for the Syndicalist union; the trend has been entirely in the opposite direction. In May, 1937, the Syndicalists tried to precipitate a strike despite the existence of a wage agreement. They felt, according to members of the other trade union, that in this way they would gain back their lost membership. A majority of workers in the mines voted not to break the agreement and the Syndicalist union has declined at an ever more rapid rate since then. If the strike had been called, of course, the company would have resorted to the labor court and in all probability would have obtained damages not only against the union but against individual members.

It is a curious community, a remote outpost of civilization built around the fabulous wealth—the iron ore is richer in content than any in the world—that lies under the two barren mountains, Kirunavaara and Luossavaara. The summer is so brief that wild flowers very rarely come into full bloom and it is only during an exceptional season that a crop of small potatoes can be harvested. The sun stands in the sky night and day for a few weeks and then the long night of winter begins to settle down.

Yes, we are well paid, the men say, but life is difficult here and we should receive higher wages. Medical care is provided at low cost under a company insurance plan. And if it is necessary to consult a specialist, the company pays for the railroad journey down to the south. Not infrequently workers put their savings in a retirement fund that will enable them to go back to a southern city and live out their old age in an environment somewhat easier, with a gayer and more diverse life. But almost as often they come back to Kiruna after a little time in the lowlands to the south. Once you have lived in the Arctic Circle, one is told, you do not want to live anywhere else.

Here, next to the North Pole as it were, with Laplanders in gaudy costume a part of the normal landscape, all the activities that characterize Swedish trade unionism go on just as in the south. The head of the Workers' Education Association at Kiruna is J. E. Westberg, the highest type of trade-union leader, serious, intelligent, giving unsparingly of his time and energy. Mr. Westberg, who is a locomotive engineer at the mines, not only has entire charge of the organization but also teaches two courses himself. In discussing the program, he stresses the effort at objectivity in the instruction given. The association offers courses in both Marxism and Nazism, trying to show, objectively, the backgrounds of both. Naturally, the teacher cannot help but show his opinions, Mr. Westberg adds. What of Nazism; will the Swedish trade unions go down before some such movement as they did in Germany? We hope, Mr. Westberg replies in slow, careful English, that our people will be so well educated that they will never accept the word of one man.

At both Boliden and Kiruna the industry is built on the exploitation of a natural resource and public good will is of vital importance. Other industries, steel and wood pulp, export industries, support towns that are just as admirable. The Norwegian Match Company has developed an independent community near Oslo that is a model of its kind.

One of the most remarkable "company towns" in Scandinavia is Sandviken where more than 5,000 men are employed by a steel company of which K. F. Göransson is the principal owner and director. Every facility for modern living has been provided and Mr. Göransson is justly proud of the community that has grown up around the works. All social services—schools, hospital, home nursing, public library, home for the aged, and so on—originally were provided by the company. Many of these functions have in later years been taken over by the community itself.

As this happened, Mr. Göransson pushed the company's program of social service into more advanced fields. In 1906 a housekeeping school for the young girls of the town was established, with expert instruction in cooking and other household skills. On the shores of a near-by lake a bathing beach and picnic ground were fitted out. The company contributed toward the Folketspark of the Metal Workers' local. It is a handsome park with gardens and shaded walks, containing a restaurant and a spacious summer theater to which each season come companies sent out from Stockholm made up of the country's leading actors. There is a central organization that sends touring companies to People's Parks in similar towns all over Sweden. Each company stays a week or ten days, doing plays of a wide variety, ranging from Shakespeare and Ibsen to modern comedy.

The latest development by the company is a huge recreation hall built in 1937 and containing an indoor tennis court, a swimming pool, a rifle range, as well as provision for other sports, including, in the basement, a large space for Boy Scouts to carry on their activities. Later an outdoor pool will be built adjoining the sports hall. Near-by is a football field and running track with bleachers. The whole town turns out to watch Sandviken's championship football teams.

Mr. Göransson is proud not only of these outward achievements but of the fact that industrial peace has prevailed for so many years at Sandviken. Collective bargaining with representatives of the union is taken for granted. It has been an accepted part of the industry for many decades. Mr. Göransson has a highly developed sense of responsibility and not only to his stockholders but to the community and the country. He is aware that as a large employer he must accept special duties and obligations. And it is not only his own personal position that is involved but the status of the employer-owner in general. I have rarely seen anyone who appears to work so hard as this man. The large house in which he lives with his wife and family is in a sense a public institution, for scarcely a week goes by that he is not host to visitors who have come to observe Sandviken. They come from all over the world to see what can be achieved when foresight and planning accompany the growth of an industry.

A community similar in some respects has come into being at Uddeholm, near the charming town of Karlstad in the province of Värmland. About 8,000 workers are employed here in the pulp mills of the Uddeholm company. But such care has been taken in the planning and the construction of the town that the green and peaceful spirit of the countryside has scarcely been disturbed. Single and two-family dwellings stand in ample ground along tree-lined streets with generous garden space. Here virtually all the houses are owned by the company. This is the lovely country made vivid to so many readers all over the globe by Selma Lagerlöf, and it is good to see that industry has touched it so lightly.

The logs for the Uddeholm mills come down the northern rivers and are floated on to Lake Vänern; they are converted into pulp and paper which are loaded directly onto the company's own ships bound for ports abroad. Uddeholm is one of Sweden's largest companies, founded on the country's three most important natural resources, forests, iron ore, and water power. The company has extensive forest lands, iron mines, and large electric power stations. Highly refined steel products, from plants located in four different communities, go all over the world.

Uddeholm is perhaps more typical than Sandviken. I do not mean to suggest that Swedish employers are all given to providing indoor tennis courts for their employees. But while the towns that I have described are exceptional in certain respects, they are not isolated phenomena. They set a standard that is generally high. The force of trade-union pressure, the influence of public opinion, persuade the employer to create a decent community, whatever his own wishes may be. There are many socially minded employers in Sweden, Norway, and Denmark and they have helped to establish the general level. But they could not have gone far without the support of aroused opinion and alert organization.

CHAPTER IX

LABOR AND THE COÖPS.

THE men and women who sit on the management council of a consumer coöperative face for the first time, the great majority of them at least, the implications of collective bargaining from the other side of the fence. In all probability, in the cities at any rate, they will belong to the trade union in the field in which they are employed. And in their respective trade unions all energy and effort have been directed toward the highest possible wage. But now in their new capacity they see wages as an element of cost in a business which they themselves are conducting, a business that is related directly to their own standard of living. This complex relationship has a number of interesting phases that bear on progress in the northern democracies.* Consumer-employers and employee-consumers have had the will to coöperate and with minor exceptions the peace has been kept.

It is not only with respect to collective bargaining that coöperative leaders sometimes find themselves in opposition to labor. In recent years sharp differences of opinion have arisen over policies formulated by the labor governments in the three countries. The general outline of a fundamental divergence can be observed and the wonder is not that there have been differences but that they have not been more frequent and more violent. Socialists in power have felt compelled to intervene increasingly in the economic life of the state; an orderly economy must be a planned economy. Coöperative leaders, on the other hand, hold to the view that their movement is a yardstick for distribution, and in a lesser degree for production, and that its effectiveness in bringing about lower prices and a higher living standard will be more or less in proportion to its freedom from interference.

* For this chapter I have drawn heavily on Mr. Herman Stolpe's excellent analysis of consumer-employee relationships contained in his book, *A New Family Economy*, published by Kooperativa Förbundet in Stockholm.

Fighting private monopoly, and oftentimes successfully, coöperators have also opposed state intervention and restriction.

This basic difference in attitude is very well illustrated in Norway at the present time. Anders Juell, chairman of Norway's central coöperative organization, Norges Kooperative Landsforening, and other leaders have vigorously opposed several important measures put forward by the present government. Particularly odious was the sales tax put over by the Laborites. Coöperators remained unconvinced by the arguments used by labor to justify such an unprecedented departure and took the traditional line of opposition to any consumption tax. Similarly, it was pointed out, coöperators had opposed a tax on tobacco when it was first proposed ten years ago by a conservative government.

In the same way the coöperative movement opposed the high import duties that have been placed on sugar, coffee, and certain other commodities. By a little simple arithmetic Mr. Juell shows what a drastic effect these tariffs have had. At the pier sugar costs 12 öre a kilogram. But when the various taxes and duties have been paid, the cost is more than four times this, about 50 öre. In the coöperative stores in the summer of 1937, the price per kilogram was 54 while in private shops it went as high as 70. In Sweden, as Mr. Juell pointed out, sugar production is a state monopoly, with imports under state control; partly this was to encourage the sugar beet industry and partly to insure a low price to consumers. A similar monopoly has been proposed in Norway but thus far it has been blocked through the power of importers with British interests a factor.

On the question of taxes Mr. Juell is a little mournful. Whatever government you have, he says, you always have new taxes. Conservative, liberal, radical, or labor, it is always taxes. In 1933 a conservative government, supported by private retail traders, put through the Parliament by a narrow margin a law taxing not only the surplus accumulated by coöperative societies but also the dividend rebated each year to consumer members. Throughout the country coöperators unleashed a powerful campaign against this law and as a result it was repealed the following year. Norwegian coöperatives now are taxed under a law passed in 1917, paying 4½ per cent on the value of property held as well as an income tax starting at 2 per cent and going up to 48 per cent on the profits that accrue on sales to non-members.

Coöperators in Norway are apprehensive over the rise in the cost of living that has taken place during the past two years. Already by July of 1937 the general index of the cost of living had passed the 1928 level which was 182, with 1914 representing 100. From January of 1937 to July of that year the index went from 176 to 187, which is a fairly rapid rise. For thirty-one towns, including Oslo, the 1928 level was 174 and the index for July of 1937 showed 169. Since then, of course, the rise has been very much slower, but nevertheless the trend continues upward.

While coöperative leaders take a stand on specific measures that concern the national economy, they insist on maintaining an attitude of political neutrality. We have to be neutral, Mr. Juell explains, because among our members are persons of all political beliefs, and particularly because we have many very small societies, often with as few as ten members, where political feeling is very strong. The central organization has worked out model rules providing that the individual societies must be politically neutral and must refrain from taking any part in political disputes. Once you begin making contributions for political purposes, you are done for, says Mr. Juell.

This is true, he adds, for a small country. Conditions in Great Britain are entirely different. In a city the size of London it is not difficult to find a half million members of approximately the same political view and on the purchasing power of a half million members a very strong coöperative movement can be built. In a small country where there are so many diverse elements the same thing is not possible. It seems to me that this is an important distinction. The Labor party does not, of course, approve the attitude of the coöperative leadership but it would not be true to say that there is any hostility between the two at the present time.

Wage negotiations between the workers in coöperative shops, factories, and warehouses are carried on with representatives of the union in the same way as in private business. In Norway these negotiations follow the line laid down in a basic agreement between the federation of labor and N.K.L., the central organization, signed at Oslo in 1936. It is almost universally true that the coöperatives pay better wages for shorter hours than private employers. There are several obvious reasons why the coöperative movement should set the standard in the wage and hour field. After all wage earners themselves make up the nucleus of the movement. In Norway they constitute nearly half of the total membership.

In Norway particularly the difference between the coöperative and the private wage scale is marked. For example, in the coöperative margarine factory there is a 44-hour week as contrasted to 48 hours in private margarine plants, with the weekly wage in the coöperative slightly higher. The coöperative employer grants two and a half weeks of vacation with pay as compared to the two weeks provided in wage contracts with private employers. Coöperative workers divide their vacation, taking two weeks in summer and a half week in winter in connection with a three-day national church holiday.

Despite the real advantages which coöperation offers as an employer, there has been occasional dissension. Not long ago, a strike was called in N.K.L.'s soap factory over wages and hours. The chief point of contention was the vacation period, with workers insisting that it should be three weeks instead of two. After six weeks the strike was settled on exactly the same terms the state arbitrator had proposed at the beginning of the conflict. The local union in the coöperative tobacco factory was prepared to call a strike over a new wage agreement, with the vacation again the chief difference. The national council of the union, however, overruled the local, holding that the agreement should be taken to arbitration with the decision of the arbitrator binding on both sides. The new agreement finally arrived at provides two and a half weeks of vacation with pay. They will all get it, says Mr. Juell, as agreements expire and new ones are made.

One thing that complicates the problem facing management councils of consumer coöperative societies is the variance in the wage level between industry and industry. It is true in general in Sweden, for example, that wages are higher in those industries which serve the domestic market than in typical export industries.

Here is a worker in a wood-pulp mill who serves on the management council of the local coöperative society. As an active trade unionist he has spent a great deal of his time and energy fighting for a higher wage scale. Now he must decide about the salaries to be paid a group of workers—shop employees—whose pay level may be considerably above his. To be sure, he may feel such a strong sense of working-class solidarity that it will give him pleasure to realize other workers have achieved a higher standard of pay. But it would be far more human for him to reason in this way: "The employees in the coöperative shops are paid largely by the industrial workers in this community. We have low wages. Why should the clerk who weighs up our flour and sugar be better paid? If the store employees get a larger income than the members generally receive, does it not mean that, unfairly, we force down the members' living standard?" This is the way in which Herman Stolpe, one of the brilliant younger men in Sweden's Coöperative Union, relates the problem to the human factor in his analysis of collective bargaining under coöperation. He adds:

In this way the management councils of the consumer societies have to wrestle with wage problems in their capacity of employer, a process which is, of course, highly instructive. Inevitably the viewpoint is broadened and the temptation to over-simplify arguments is reduced. It can be fairly stated that collective bargaining between labor and employer in Sweden is carried out on a very high plane of enlightened opinion. This is undoubtedly explained by the fact that labor and men and women on small salaries have learned through the consumer societies to look upon the wage problem not only in the light of self-interest but as an element of cost in goods distributed and consumed.

The whole problem, as Mr. Stolpe points out, is seen from another perspective. It is far less simple than it appeared from the trade-union side of the conference table. In a coöperative enterprise functioning under the control of consumer members there are no capitalists whose "undeserved profits" can be reduced by increasing wages; such an increase is immediately reflected in higher prices to the consumers.

Local coöperative societies in Sweden have more than 14,000 employees and their annual wage bill is approximately $27,-500,000. In relation to gross sales the percentage paid out in wages has nearly doubled in the years from 1918 to 1935, going from 3.4 per cent to 6.7. There would be reason for consumers to be alarmed about this trend, Mr. Stolpe points out, were it not for the fact that a rationalization of the whole distributive trade has taken place during that period, thanks largely to the efficient methods introduced by the coöperatives. That consumer societies can pay better salaries is not surprising when it is realized that on the average the sales volume is 100 per cent higher and the sales per employee 50 per cent larger than in the private stores. A capable, well-trained personnel has contributed not a little to this result, according to Mr. Stolpe.

The principal training school is Vår Gård, organized and conducted by the Coöperative Union at Saltsjöbaden, near Stockholm. Short courses at Vår Gård, from one week to a month, come as a conclusion to studies pursued by correspondence. The young clerk behind the counter takes courses by mail in window-display, lettering, bookkeeping, and other subjects of immediate use in his job. If his response to these courses is good, then he is allowed to go to Vår Gård for a week. The local society usually contributes to his expenses, the cost of the course being only 40 kronor. Naturally in so short a time he cannot absorb a great deal of knowledge but he comes back to his job full of new ideas and impressions, to resume study by correspondence. If he is promoted to store manager, he returns to Vår Gård for a special course for managers which lasts a month. This course is offered free and is in the nature of a reward for those who have made good records in their earlier studies.

The school, like so many other institutions in Sweden, combines a great deal of hard work with the opportunity for an exchange of ideas and the facilities for sport and recreation. The principal building is the one-time mansion of a man of property, beautifully situated in wooded grounds and looking over an inlet of the Baltic. Bathing and sailing in summer and skiing and ice skating in winter are outside activities that add not a little to the attractiveness of Vår Gård.

One of the most interesting courses offered is that in which young clerks and store managers are taught the difference between good simple design in ordinary things and bad taste, superfluity of ornament, and useless detail. There is a kind of laboratory in which the good and the bad are put side by side: china, furniture, packages of tea and coffee, textiles. Changed from time to time under the supervision of the staff of architects employed by the Coöperative Union, these examples of right and wrong are a forceful object lesson in themselves. Another course has to do with the arrangement, for efficiency and attractiveness, of store interiors.

Besides the 14,000 workers on the pay rolls of local coöperative societies, the Coöperative Union employs nearly 5,000 men and women, in a variety of fields of manufacture and distribution; technicians in the lamp factory, general labor at docks and warehouses, accountants and stenographers, foremen and skilled craftsmen. As in the retail trade carried on by consumer societies, the wage standard for the respective occupation or trade is taken as the basis of bargaining with coöperative employees. To this base certain advantages are invariably added in wage contracts signed with the union.

For example, in the coöperative shoe factory piecework rates are from 20 to 25 per cent higher than in private factories. Workers in the coöperative flour mill, Three Crowns, at Stockholm, are paid 68 kronor for a 48-hour week; they get 12 days' vacation with full pay; and they receive half pay during illness up to 120 days. In a comparable private mill the wage is 65 kronor; the vacation (this was prior to the recent law) is 6 days; and half pay during illness is granted for only 90 days. In contrast, as Mr. Stolpe points out, executive salaries in the Coöperative Union are considerably lower than in private industry. Albin Johansson, managing director of this extensive enterprise, receives a salary of 20,000 kronor a year. Technical experts are an exception to this generalization, however, since they must be paid at the going rate.

Besides being a model employer in most respects, the Union has in two or three instances gone in for housing for coöperative workers. The architectural staff has designed housing projects in connection with two or three enterprises and the union has made it possible for employees to buy these well-built but inexpensive houses. The most conspicuous example is the colony created for workers at the Three Crowns Mill, laid out on a slope in such a way that each house has a splendid view out over Stockholm harbor.

Mr. Stolpe writes:

This regard for the personnel must not obscure the real purpose of consumer coöperation which is to protect the *consumers'* interest in every possible way. After all the Coöperatives are in competition with private business and they can succeed only if prices in co-operative stores compare favorably with those in other stores. Co-operative employees cannot, therefore, expect to receive salaries and wages which would prevent efficient competition and thereby undermine the foundation of the movement.

Unfortunately not all coöperative employees have a clear under-standing of this direct relationship between their salaries and wages on the one hand and the prices of distributed and manufactured goods on the other. That such a direct relationship exists must be obvious to any unbiased observer. This is even more obvious in the coöperative retail trade where wages are not less than 70 per cent of total expenditures. Nevertheless there has been one strike in a coöperative factory, despite the fact that workers in this factory were receiving higher wages than a private factory nearby was paying.

Neither the Coöperative Union nor any of the local societies hold membership in the Employers' Association. Mr. Stolpe points to the independent course that coöperators have followed in all fields and naturally, he adds, they would take an inde-pendent line here, too. What is more, of course, the whole basis of operation is different and there would be no common ground.

The link between the coöperatives and the trade unions has always been close. They have grown up together, recruiting their members for the most part from the same class. Virtually all coöperative employees are enrolled in unions. To lessen the possibility of conflict there was set up some years ago a special arbitration board made up of an equal number of representa-tives of the Coöperative Union and the federation of labor. If a collective agreement cannot be reached by negotiation, both sides must submit their proposals to the arbitration board be-fore any measure of force is resorted to. More important perhaps, this board passes upon all disputes arising while wage contracts are in force. Since it was established in 1926, Mr. Stolpe writes, the board has functioned to the satisfaction of both parties and virtually all disagreements have been settled through this means.

Although this link is so close I did not find any trade unionists in Sweden who resented the independence of the coöperatives. There seemed to be a fairly clear realization of the fact that consumer coöperation is built upon the membership of all classes so that today all groups are represented in more or less the same proportion as in the general population. In the course of a conversation with a young trade-union leader about the relationship between the two movements he had this to say: "No, of course, the coöperative could not help in the event of a strike; that would be against the rules. All the coöperatives in Sweden follow the principle of detachment from political questions. Since they enroll all classes it would not be fair to help one class."

Inherent in the gradual growth of the coöperative movement to its present strength is an accretion of political and economic power that is very real regardless of the fact that it has seldom been brought to bear on immediate issues. Now and then it has been ranged against the labor party. This opposition was most conspicuous when, prior to the 1936 election, the Laborites proposed to extend the system of state monopolies to new fields in order to raise additional revenue to increase old-age pensions. Specifically they proposed to make the importation and distribution of gasoline and certain kinds of medicine a monopoly of the state.

This was directly counter to the economic philosophy of Albin Johansson who has directed not a little of the energy of the movement that he heads into the fight on private monopoly. As he conceives it, the chief function of coöperation is to insure free competition and thereby promote the distribution of goods at the lowest possible cost. Public monopoly is no less an evil than private monopoly in his view. Mr. Johansson announced his determined opposition to the government's proposals. It had been thought that the monopoly question would be an important factor in the campaign but shortly afterward the whole issue was dropped, as a result, in part at least, of Mr. Johansson's statement. Another factor was the threat of a "Red scare" from Conservative and Liberal sources at this suggestion to extend the economic controls of the government.

There is not, as this shows, complete agreement on policy and program between labor and the coöperatives. How sharp the conflict might become in the event of a split over a major issue is a matter of speculation. Certainly Mr. Johansson's views are far more conservative and more cautious in many respects than those of party leaders such as Ernst Wigforss. On the other hand Mr. Johansson has pushed at every opportunity the coöperative ownership of the means of production, constantly venturing into new fields whenever it has seemed possible to reduce prices and improve quality.

In Denmark coöperation has for the most part been from the producers' side. The direction has been rural rather than urban and any political influence coöperators may have exerted has been on behalf of farm groups. The working relationship with the trade unions has been the same as in Sweden and Norway but the fundamental differences setting the two movements apart have been greater. Negotiations with coöperative slaughterhouses and bacon factories have been on virtually the same basis as with an ordinary private employer.

Nowhere in Scandinavia has this issue of wages between labor and the coöperatives really been settled. Recently in *Vi,* the magazine of Sweden's Coöperative Union with the largest circulation of any publication in the country, an article appeared suggesting that wages of coöperative employees should be leveled downward in regions where the coöperative scale was higher than the industrial scale. The writer argued that this was in line with a new uniform wage policy announced by the National Federation of Labor. This was promptly challenged in the monthly journal of the Retail Workers' Union. If this were to be the policy, the union said in reply, then in many other areas wages would have to be greatly increased.

The article in the union journal questioned the claim of coöperative leaders that wage scales are higher in consumer-owned shops. In both private and coöperative stores, according to the trade union's analysis, the wages of women clerks are on the same level. Women office workers are paid somewhat less by the coöperatives than by private business. Wages for men working in coöperative shops seem to be higher but, according to the union, this was only because store managers were included, bringing up the average considerably. In arriving at the average for private business, the article pointed out, store managers are not included.

An undercurrent of dissatisfaction is reflected in this. At the 1934 convention of the Retail Workers' Union several motions were offered asking for the abolition of the board of arbitration that passes upon wage agreements between employees and coöperative employers. Possibly it is true, coöperative workers say, that we receive somewhat more generous compensation than men and women in private trade. But this does not mean very much if our wage rate is appreciably under that of the industrial average in many of the communities where we are employed. Certainly it is true that the coöperative average—about 200 kronor a month—does not compare favorably with the national industrial average. The answer lies, according to objective observers, not so much in greater discriminations in favor of coöperative employees as in stronger retail trade unions that will improve the position of all the workers in this field.

CHAPTER X

WHITE-COLLAR TRADE UNIONS

PERSUADING the white-collar worker that his interests are with labor and that his hope for security and a higher wage lies in belonging to a union is a task that is just now absorbing a great deal of energy and thought in the three Scandinavian countries. There is no field of trade-union organization on which greater stress is placed. The example of Germany, where the lower middle class went over almost en bloc to the Right, would be compelling if no other reason existed for enrolling this important group of wage earners.

In Denmark at least it has been realized that this cannot be done merely by invocation of the old symbols. Workers of the world unite, etc., has no inherent power to attract the bank clerk or the insurance actuary. An invitation to join the proletariat works no magic on the little man who is struggling to maintain his family in a modest suburb. These people have a middle-class psychology and the union appeal must be presented to them in those terms.

This is just what the Commercial and Business Helpers' Union in Denmark is trying to do, employing the most modern methods of mass advertising. At the beginning of an intensive drive for membership, the union engaged the services of a large advertising firm so that the appeal would be as effective as possible. By pictures, posters, motion picture films, direct by mail, in all the variety of ways known to the resourceful copy writer, Denmark's white-collar class has been urged to belong to a trade union.

The advantages inherent in organization were translated into terms understandable to office workers occupying the precarious economic limbo that is reserved for the lower middle class. A young man and his girl find they can't marry because his salary is so low; they learn after a quarrel that if his office is organized it will be possible to demand, and, in all probability, obtain a substantial increase; happiness and hope dawn at the end of a dialogue presented in a brochure with amusing drawings. Another brochure sent to a large mailing list and distributed in offices and shops is of the testimonial type, with endorsements by pretty girls who tell what the union has done for them, what it has meant in vacations, clothes, and so on.

Whenever possible the campaign was connected with the news, a best seller, or a popular play. Hans Fallada's novel, *Little Man, What Now?* was a great success in Denmark. Permission was obtained to print the first thirty or forty pages, describing the plight of the luckless little man, in a broadside. Then, where the story breaks off, the union presents its "answer" to the troubles of all such little men and women. Only through organization, the strength that comes out of union for a common purpose, can the little men be saved; this was the union thesis. Thousands of copies of the broadside were given away at the theater that showed the film made from the Fallada novel.

Some of the most effective propaganda has been based on the vacations at cost to be enjoyed at the union's two seaside vacation homes. "What is in the traveling bag?" is the caption scribbled on the outside of a pamphlet printed to look like a strapped and labeled handbag. Inside are the symbols of health, beauty, leisure, all to be had at Strandhus or Borshøjgaard for those who are fortunate enough to belong to the union. Picture postal cards representing the vacation houses in glowing colors bear a printed message on the back addressed to "Dear Colleague," describing the pleasures of vacation life, all to be had, it is made clear, through union membership.

Other pamphlets and posters make a more direct appeal. "Twenty-five thousand coworkers are with you" one is captioned. The Commercial and Business Helpers' Union, it sets forth, can obtain better working conditions, higher wages, and pay for overtime. What is perhaps most striking about all this propaganda is the way in which it is addressed to youth and the desires of youth. Small stickers heralding the annual convention show a white outline map of the country on an orange background with the photographs of three young people, a young man in plus fours with a banjo-guitar, a pretty girl, and another young man, superimposed.

The net effect of all this is attractive and appealing and there is no doubt that it has had a great deal to do with the union's rapid growth in recent years. Other factors have entered but there is no question of the influence that has been exerted by the constant stream of propaganda which has come from the union's principal offices in Copenhagen. Just after the World War as a result of the brief spurt of prosperity that came then, the white-collar union, along with all others, enjoyed a sudden influx of membership. From 1920 onward there was a fairly rapid decline until 1927 when for that year and the four succeeding years slight increases were recorded.

The real incentive to growth came, however, in 1932 when the union affiliated with the central federation of trade unions. The question of affiliation had long been a source of dissension within the union. It had been up at two of the congresses that are held every four years and twice the decision was to refer it to the membership for a general vote. On both occasions the vote was against affiliation. Leaders of the union felt strongly that there could be no real growth until the link was made with the labor movement as a whole. Therefore the congress in 1932 voted to affiliate without reference to the membership. The membership has increased since that time from 16,000 to nearly 30,000 at the end of 1937, and leaders are hopeful that this growth will continue.

Thus far white-collar workers in Denmark have been involved in only one major conflict. That was with a large insurance company in Copenhagen and the consequences were unfortunate. After the breakdown of wage negotiations, several hundred office workers went on strike. The company promptly hired an entire new staff and ultimately the strikers were compelled to seek new jobs. First of all, there was an abundant supply of stenographers and accountants outside the ranks of the union on which the company could draw. But more important, there was no way to make a boycott effective since the basis of the firm's business was re-insurance with other companies. The strike enlisted the support of virtually all organized labor but there was no way in which this force could be brought to bear on the side of the strikers.

The union, as leaders themselves are very well aware, has a

long way to go. Only about 33 to 35 per cent of all office workers are organized. Each year about 2,000 names are dropped from union lists, those who marry and give up work or change to a trade. The forces of organized labor, now united behind the union through the central federation, must enlist a much larger proportion of white-collar workers if the political and social effect on the middle class is to be of any importance. White-collar trade unions in Germany were comparatively strong before Hitler. In fact they made up the largest part of the membership of the international organization of office and allied workers. The unions affiliated to this international had at one time a combined membership of more than one million. This dropped to about 400,000 after the Nazis came into power. It is now back to nearly 600,000, due almost entirely to increases in Great Britain and Scandinavia. An effort is being made to strengthen the international tie and visiting delegates are frequently interchanged between the various countries that now contribute the greater part of the membership.

In Sweden as in Denmark there is a strong determination to increase the ranks of organized white-collar workers although the situation in the more northerly country is quite different. An evolutionary process is taking place in Sweden. White-collar groups that have hitherto looked askance at trade-union tactics are being transformed by force of circumstance, with the encouragement of industrial unions in the federation of labor.

These white-collar groups have for many years been affiliated to a separate federation, known from the initials of the principal organizations comprising it as DACO. Everyone expects that some day DACO will be combined with the trade-union federation but there is also a general belief that it would be a mistake to hasten this union. The feeling is that many of the groups in DACO are not yet ready to take the final step into trade unionism. Between the two central organizations a mutually helpful understanding exists despite the fact that there have been jurisdictional differences in the past, notably over rival efforts to organize shop clerks.

DACO is made up of a number of different groups. Included among those with the largest membership are the Industrial Clerks' Union, the Foremen's Union, the Commercial Workers'

Union, the Union of Railway Office Personnel, the Bank Employees' Union, Association of Restaurant and Hotel Clerks, the Business Machine Operators' Union, and the Association of Agricultural Engineers' Assistants. Besides this there is an association of ship commanders, of maîtres d'hôtel, of architectural draftsmen.

It is obvious that among such diverse groups there would be marked difference of opinion with respect to the use of straightforward trade-union tactics. The shop foremen's union, for example, follows a very conservative policy. There are groups within DACO, however, and among them the largest and most influential, that have the trade-union point of view. The Bank Employees' Union is one of these. Leaders of the union have taken several recent occasions to declare publicly, and in no uncertain terms, that their organization is a trade union which in every instance is prepared to follow trade-union tactics. By those responsible for shaping policy it has been felt that the wisest course was not to force the issue of trade unionism since the trend in virtually all groups was in that direction.

White-collar workers in Sweden have in late years become acutely aware of the need for organization. Their wage scale has been low, in many instances lower than that of skilled workers under trade-union contracts. They have failed to obtain the benefits granted by such wage contracts and they have been, as individuals, far more insecure in their jobs. Realizing all this they have come to recognize the need for organized collective bargaining. The vague "respectability" which they had clung to, as office workers independent of the kind of organization uniting the men in the shop, was not enough to compensate for wages so low that they barely met the living expenses of husband and wife.

Nevertheless for the office worker it is a new adventure, this business of collective bargaining, and he approaches it at first with some timidity. Here is a large office employing several hundred stenographers and accountants. By months of painstaking work a large majority of the force has been organized, partly with the aid of DACO but largely through those who have already come to assume leadership in the new union. A committee is appointed to formulate a set of demands. After long discussion at a meeting of the union the committee's report is agreed to as a basis for action. A lengthy letter is drawn up and finally presented by a committee to the management.

In all probability the reaction to this first demand may be unfavorable. Employers have long been accustomed to bargaining collectively with their workers in the shop; the pattern for this is familiar and accepted. But such a demand coming from the men and women in the office is new and startling. The management decides, for the time being at least, to say nothing. When the union committee presents a second letter, the curt reply comes back that the demands will not be met. The next step for the union is, of course, to turn to DACO. And from here on the central organization takes over the negotiations. DACO is powerful and the company cannot ignore its demands for a conference. The discussion, which is carried on by impersonal representatives, will end in a contract. And while this contract will not contain everything that was originally asked for, it will be an excellent start.

DACO's rise is being closely watched by leaders of the Labor party and the trade-union movement who are lending aid and counsel whenever it is feasible. Two or three intelligent younger men have been placed in positions of influence. But, what is more important, the trade-union federation has arranged to cooperate with the Commercial Workers' Union in the organization of clerks and office employees in industry. The particular union enrolling the workers in the shop will collaborate with the white-collar union in organizing the front office. It is not difficult to foresee the time when a merger will be possible so that all employees in an industry, from the expert accountant to the lowliest sweeper, will belong to the same organization.

At a recent meeting of DACO's board of directors it was decided to get together a fund for building up the union. Representatives of all the larger groups were present at this meeting and agreed upon an active policy of development. Reviewing the year just past, the chairman could point to a larger measure of success than ever before in the history of the organization. There was considerable discussion as to how to bring the various unions closer together, particularly in regard to a solution of their common problems. Approval was given to continuation of the joint committee made up of representatives of the trade-union federation and DACO which is seeking ways to strengthen the relationship between the two. The chairman had been E. Ahlberg of the Foremen's Union. For the reason that he could not give so much time to the office he declined reëlection and Captain Gunnar Osvald of the Ship Commanders' Association was named in his place.

Many professional and semiprofessional groups are outside of DACO. Journalists are closely organized in what is the equivalent of a trade union but their organization is not affiliated to any federation. Thus far there has been no concerted move to include these isolated groups. It would seem probable that some day they would all be drawn into either DACO or the trade-union federation.

One can look forward to the time when, if there are no major interruptions, the whole labor movement, including the white-collar class, will be unified within a single general federation. There is no great concern over when this will come about since the relationship between the two central organizations is excellent. It is, rather, an expectation of the not too distant future to which everyone looks forward with a large degree of certainty.

CHAPTER XI

IN CONCLUSION

THE fact remains, when all the painstaking arrangements for collective bargaining have been reviewed, that the Scandinavian countries have had during the past decade the highest record of man-days lost through industrial conflict in the world. So many aspects of the employer-employee relationship are favorable to peace in industry that this seems strikingly paradoxical. What are the reasons? Why should there be so many strikes and lockouts in a part of the world where so much forethought and planning have gone into the process of collective bargaining?

First of all, it is important to consider that the phase of development of trade unionism in Scandinavia is closely related to the industrial development of the three countries and that this fact has a bearing on the type of industrial relations that prevail. The whole process of industrialization began much later than in Great Britain and on the continent. Similarly the cycle of trade-union development has lagged behind that of the rest of Europe. For all the gains that have been won by the trade unions since 1920, it has nevertheless remained true that there have been within the labor movement unassimilated and at times hostile elements. The strikes of the past ten years, in Sweden and Norway at any rate, may be related to a process of unification, of assimilation, that has taken place. Radical and reformist elements have now become more or less reconciled. That phase, one may say with some degree of confidence, is at an end.

This raises a larger question as to trade-union evolution. Does trade unionism in its rise and fall merely follow the cycle of industrialization? In this connection a comparison with the statistics for other countries is interesting. As was pointed out in the introduction, Norway was first with 3,176 man-days lost per thousand workers in industry as a result of wage disputes, Sweden next with 1,818 days, Denmark third with an average of

935, this for the decade from 1927 through 1936. Australia ranks fourth with an average of 871, and the United States fifth with 791. Japan is at the bottom with only 104 lost days a year on the average for the period covered. And of course there are no figures on industrial conflicts for the dictator nations—Russia, Germany, and Italy.

In Great Britain there were comparatively few wage disputes, the ten-year average of man-days lost being only 333 per thousand workers. Does this mean, one may ask, that labor in Britain is no longer on the aggressive? Of course, no such conclusion can be drawn. Yet a glance at the postwar history of the British labor movement, particularly since the critical year of 1926 (if that year had been included, the British average would have been quite different), must lead to the conclusion that a kind of stalemate has come about.

Real wages in Great Britain have shown little or no gain in the past decade. And while a solid nucleus of labor votes has been held around the trade unions, the Labor party has tended more and more to become a kind of permanent official opposition, without any real hope of coming into power. In short, there has been a retreat instead of a forward march and the contrast with Scandinavian experience has been striking. As has been said, this suggests a parallel between the process of industrialization and the cycle of the trade-union movement.

It is of no little significance that labor leaders in Scandinavia are aware of the possibility of such a parallel; that the graph of the rise of trade unionism merely follows the growth of industry and, correspondingly, declines with it. Certainly they show practical wisdom in realizing that the self-centered pressure tactics which may be successful in a fast-developing industrial system must be supplemented at this stage by coöperative efforts with other groups.

As I have tried to show, leaders in Scandinavia are striving to broaden and expand the whole labor movement. They are trying to arrive at a unified wage policy whereby the wage scales of those at the bottom will be brought more nearly in line with those at the top. They are trying to draw in a large part of the middle class. They are working toward real collaboration with farm workers. They are seeking to avoid the blight of institutionalism, of bureaucracy, of the kind of officialdom that is interested merely in conserving a vested interest. And they are studying ways in which they may collaborate with management in the production of a larger national income, of which the strength of their organization will win for them a fair share. In all this is the hope of continued growth; the hope that the present period of strength and prosperity is not merely a phase that will inevitably be followed by retrogression and decay.

There are, to be sure, certain large problems as yet unsolved. Conspicuous among these is the problem of the building industry, particularly in relation to the building-craft unions. Strikes and lockouts in the building industry were largely responsible for the high average that the Scandinavian countries show in the study of wage conflicts. Prolonged strikes occurred in 1930, 1931, and 1932 in the building industry.

A government committee has just completed a nationwide report on construction which includes recommendations for increased governmental control through a central building board. This board would have power to coördinate building activity, not only public but private, looking toward a leveling-out of seasonal highs and lows. Public building of the central government, counties, and towns would be brought under some rational and unified plan so that it would be spaced out with reference to employment. The committee also recommended that a thoroughgoing study be made of the monopolistic effect of both employer and employee organizations and suggested an investigation under the 1925 monopoly law of monopolistic price controls in the building materials industry. While the report does not go far, it is at least a beginning looking toward more drastic recommendations in the near future.

The degree to which labor leaders coöperate with employers, not only over the immediate ends of collective bargaining but with respect to the whole pattern of the economy is a phenomenon that never fails to impress the visitor from America. As I have tried to make clear, it seems to me that this comes out of the confidence that has grown up between the two sides. Employers have come to accept collective bargaining without any reservations whatsoever. They do not enter into it with the thought that it is merely a temporary expedient, an unnecessary evil that can be eliminated when the power of the trade union has been destroyed once and for all.

I do not think that the importance of this can be overstressed. It is why the relationships described in the chapter "Company Town" can exist without the suspicion of an ulterior paternalism. The "company town" is not contrived to hold the workers in bondage. And the Employers' Association exists not for breaking strikes or providing industrial spies but for the primary purpose of carrying out collective bargaining.

For their part, the trade-union representatives come to the bargaining conference with a realistic appreciation of the task at hand. Leaders have deviated but little from the line of practical, hardheaded trade unionism, never losing sight of the tangible gains to the rank and file that must be the basis of any solid and coherent labor movement. Sitting around the conference table, they have had no illusions that a socialist millennium was to be achieved through a gain of two crowns a week. Social and political theory has had a definite function but it has never been allowed to obscure the immediate objective.

When two groups with vital interests in the proportionate share of each in a joint product are strongly organized, as in Scandinavia, one expects that concessions will not be made without a struggle and possibly with a show of power as the ultimate argument. Yet it cannot be denied that both groups have helped to develop a machinery for collective bargaining which reduces such instances below the number normally to be expected in periods of rapid industrial growth paralleled by rapid and successful growth in organized power on both sides of the bargaining table.

Now, as I have tried to point out, trade unionists have come up against the realization that very possibly a limit has been reached in the size of the share of the national income that labor can obtain by present tactics and within the limits of the present economy. It is more or less clearly understood that if labor's share is to be increased, then production must be greatly expanded. And trade-union heads have said, in effect: We will work to that end, we will coöperate, but in return you must recognize that we are partners in the real meaning of the word and therefore entitled to a voice in management. What is more, the basic insecurity under which we work does not accord with a true partnership and we must therefore come to a new and better understanding.

That is the line that labor is following today. It is a bold and venturesome line and one can scarcely predict what ultimately will come of it. The high type of trade-union leadership prevailing in the Scandinavian countries encourages the belief that real achievements will come out of this new approach; that it is the beginning of a new era of collective bargaining in an expanded sphere and not a dead end.

Above all, that is the impression which remains—the high seriousness of the men and women who head the labor movement in the north of Europe. Acutely aware of the gravity of the task they face in a changing world, they bring to the jobs they do from day to day a kind of selflessness, an intensity of interest, yes, a devotion, that transcends mere careerism. Realizing the limitations inherent in old forms—in the narrow, craft concept—they are struggling to find new forms adapted to an industrial civilization. It is not easy. There is the dead weight of inertia, of prejudice, of ancient self-interest. But if this experiment in industrial democracy is not upset by the disaster of war, it may well bring achievements that will have significance for democracy everywhere.

INDEX

ARY
versity

Date Due

Jan 15'43			
Mar 30 '43			
Mar 31'43			
Jan 20'48			